REMARKABLE
RACECOURSES

Pavilion
An imprint of HarperCollins*Publishers*
1 London Bridge Street
London SE1 9GF

www.harpercollins.co.uk

HarperCollins*Publishers*
Macken House
39/40 Mayor Street Upper
Dublin 1
D01 C9W8
Ireland

ISBN 978-1-911216-87-2

A CIP catalogue record for this book is available from
the British Library.

10 9 8 7 6 5 4 3 2

Reproduction by Rival UK

Printed and bound by GPS Group in Bosnia and Herzegovina

This book can be ordered direct from the publisher at
www.pavilionbooks.com

This book is produced from independently certified FSC™ paper
to ensure responsible forest management.

For more information visit: www.harpercollins.co.uk/green

Acknowledgements:

I often remind myself how lucky I have been to have a job that is
also my hobby, and a combination of the two meant that I have
already been to nearly half of the racecourses that appear in
the book. I have been inspired to attend many more, with the
threatened Beirut Hippodrome and the hilltop track at Zonza in
Corsica high on my list, and I hope that readers will feel the same.

There are plenty of people to thank, not least my parents, James
and Harriet Peacock, for being the first sub-editing safety net, and
Frank Hopkinson for commissioning me.

Contacts from around the world of racing helped with suggestions
and information. I would like to place on record my thanks to
Marcus Armytage, Edward Prosser, Emma Berry, Isabel Mathew,
Joe Kristufek, Kate Hunter, Howard Wright, Dr Carlo Zuccoli,
Jeremy Grayson, Jane Rogan, Paul Bloodworth, Gary Mudgway,
Shona Dreaper and Sally Henery.

Books not already acknowledged that were of particular use
were: *The Kentucky Derby, Preakness and Belmont Stakes: A
Comprehensive History* by Richard Sowers. *Belmont Park: A
Century of Champions* and *Crown Jewels of Thoroughbred Racing*
by Richard Stone Reeves. *Racecourse Architecture* by Paul Roberts
and Isabelle Taylor.

REMARKABLE
RACECOURSES

— TOM PEACOCK —

FOREWORD BY MARCUS ARMYTAGE

PAVILION

Contents

Foreword

Horseracing is a remarkable sport. It has been going on, in one form or another, for millennia and for those who hold it dear to their hearts it is a passport to the world; for there are few countries where it does not exist at some level, and there are few places where the ardent racegoer or horseman will not be received with open arms.

Racing transcends most of the world's notional barriers and borders be they religious, political, racial, lingual or geographical which means there are a vast array of racecourses.

One of the great things about the sport of kings is that, unlike one of the world's other universal pastimes, football; where a pitch is determined by a uniform set of measurements and is the same in Korea as it is in the London suburbs, there are no rules governing a racecourse's layout or situation.

The vast majority are deeply rooted in history. Seldom does a Royal Ascot pass without reference to how the prescient Queen Anne, on a hunting trip from Windsor Castle, happened upon an area of heath which she thought suitable for racing.

The Goodwood Cup, for example, was established in 1808 – over two hundred years ago – on an area where the Duke of Richmond let the local militia race their horses, while the famous fences at Aintree, which at first glance appear skewed at odd angles across the course, actually follow the old hedge lines from when Aintree was a rural parish with more plough than grass, and the race was over what was termed natural country.

An actual racecourse itself can be left-handed, right-handed or, indeed, in some cases a mixture of both; although those in America are invariably left-handed. Some, like Newmarket, are straight; some boast long sweeping galloping turns, others are so tight they test a horse's ability to corner. In the latter respect the Palio di Siena is out on its own.

They can host Flat or jump racing and they need not necessarily be level. Indeed Epsom, host of the most famous Flat race in the world, the Derby, is one of the hilliest. There are few limits, it seems, to the surface providing it is safe for

RIGHT: Cartmel racecourse in Cumbria.
PREVIOUS PAGE: A night meeting at Meydan, Dubai.

horses to gallop upon from the 'White Turf' – ice and snow – of St Moritz, to the low-tide beach at Laytown in Ireland, to the various dirt mixtures in America, to the man-made synthetic surfaces of the modern 'all-weather', but nothing beats glorious green turf.

I have been lucky to visit many of the courses included by Tom Peacock in *Remarkable Racecourses* as racegoer, racing correspondent for the *Daily Telegraph* and, thanks mainly to representing Britain in the late 1980s and early 1990s in the Fegentri (International Federation of Gentlemen and Lady Amateur Riders) Championship which was then expanding from its European origins to America and the rest of the world, ride at quite a few of them too.

My first Fegentri ride was in 1987 in Pardubice, in a mile-and-three-quarter novice hurdle in what was then communist Czechoslovakia. I was picked up at the airport by the local racing secretary and driven in his rickety Trabant through a deserted and dark Prague, a city then untouched by Western Europe, untouched, apparently, by electricity and where the prospect of a jolly stag party was unimaginable. There was neither a light on nor an advertising hoarding and it was the closest I had been to driving through a Graham Greene novel.

Though unable to speak a word of Czech I was made to feel very welcome and witnessed, for the first time, the Velka Pardubicka, then known as the Iron Curtain's Grand National. The Trabant made it back to Prague but did not quite make it up the hill to the airport, breaking down two furlongs short of the terminal with steam pouring from the boot which was where the engine sat. In 1990 I returned for the first of three rides in the great race on Czech-trained horses.

My first ever ride was at Newmarket's July course where I went considerably faster to the start than I did on the way back. At Punchestown I got no

further than the seventh, a drop bank, in the La Touche, while at Aintree I have experienced both sides of the coin; the glory of winning and the utter disappointment of falling at the first.

In St. Moritz, where it was about -10 C I waited in the 'paddock' wearing only my silk colours and light breeches because I was struggling with the weight and narrowly averted hypothermia.

At La Zarzuela, Madrid, I rode for my childhood hero, the Beltran, the 18th Duque de Albuquerque whose failed attempts to win the Grand National inspired me to become an amateur jockey, while at Waregem in Belgium I likened their Flanders National the equivalent of riding a race around Badminton – not for the faint-hearted.

It is the trend these days for people to attempt to visit every racecourse in Britain or wherever, be that by foot, bicycle or car. The beauty of *Remarkable Racecourses* is that you can visit 88 of the world's most interesting racecourses without leaving the comfort of your armchair. Good luck with your journey.

Marcus Armytage, September 2017

RIGHT: Pardubice's giant fence Taxis is No.4 on the course. BELOW: A complete contrast to the lush scenery of the Czech Republic, the Birdsville Races are held in the middle of the Simpson Desert in Queensland.

Aintree

Merseyside, England

The presence of arguably the world's most famous horse race on its most iconic racecourse should never be taken for granted. Back in the 1970s, the Grand National appeared in peril. The Topham family, who ran Aintree for many years, sold the site to the property developer Bill Davies and despite assertions to the contrary, there were regular rumours that this green space on the edge of Liverpool would be turned over to the diggers.

Attendance in 1975 was the smallest ever, partly due to exorbitant admission prices, and it was only the intervention of Ladbrokes bookmakers, as overseeing sponsors, that the race was revived and its future was finally safeguarded when acquired by Jockey Club Racecourses in 1983.

Not that it has been smooth sailing ever since. In the glare of a large and global television audience there have been equine fatalities, the false start that many of the riders failed to notice in 1993 and the 1997 evacuation from an IRA bomb threat.

Under the 25-year chairmanship of Lord Daresbury, a Cheshire man who was an outstanding amateur rider but fell at the first fence on his only attempt at the National, the race has perked up yet again. Prize money has reached record levels and facilities were gradually upgraded through the openings of the Queen Mother and Princess Royal Stands in the 1990s.

In 2007 a final makeover was completed by the award-winning architects BDP of the Earl of Derby and Lord Sefton Stands, in wood, concrete and glass. The cramped old winner's enclosure, where successful riders virtually had to duck down to prevent banging their heads on the roof, has been turned into a bar, and now many thousands can welcome the victors back into a modern open-air amphitheatre.

The three-day National meeting attracts a total of 150,000 punters in early April and has become an important date in the diary for the citizens of the north-west. Most arrive dressed to the nines, with many in very little for the time of year.

Aintree does hold other races and meetings over hurdles and a conventional parkland steeplechase track known as the Mildmay

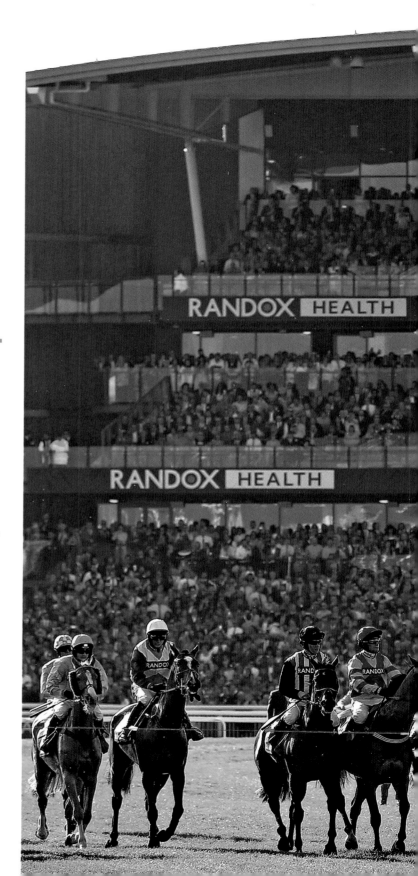

EARL OF DERBY STAND
ANDOX HEALTH
RANDOX HEALTH
RANDOX HEALTH
OX HEALTH GRAND NATIONAL
RANDOX HEALTH

Course, a particularly tight and fast circuit with fences that will catch out any dubious jumper, but it is famed for the Grand National Course.

A separate track of around two and a quarter miles, used for just five contests per year, it has 16 distinctive green fences. Many of them have names derived from the days when they were far more formidable obstacles, such as Valentine's Brook and the Canal Turn.

The Chair, in front of the stands, is the biggest at 5 ft 2 in (1.57 metres), while Becher's Brook used to be the most dangerous. It had an enormous drop on the landing side and is named after Captain Mark Becher, who fell in the first running of 1839 and remained hiding in the brook as the rest of the field passed over.

Foinavon, the fence after Becher's, is neither the largest nor the trickiest but in 1967 it was the scene of a pile-up that its namesake was the only horse to avoid, and went on to win at 100-1. Many other incidents have become knitted into the race's folklore, no more so than when The Queen Mother's horse Devon Loch mysteriously flopped onto his stomach with the 1956 National at his mercy, possibly jumping a shadow or an imaginary fence. His jockey Dick Francis went on to phenomenal success with his novels of racing skulduggery.

The National's greatest equine hero was Red Rum, trained on the beach at nearby Southport in the 1970s by Ginger McCain. Red Rum even ran at Aintree as a two-year-old when it still staged Flat meetings and the marathon's only three-time winner is buried next to the winning post.

The field start the four and a half miles and two circuits of the National away from the stands, cross the Melling Road, and head off into 'the country'. This backdrop is hardly that of a rural John Constable landscape, given that Aintree is

PREVIOUS PAGE: Horses line up at the start of the 2017 Randox Health Grand National.

BELOW: Riders turn sharp left at the Canal Turn.

BOTTOM: Horses and riders take the first bend in one of the Grand National's support races, the Gaskells Handicap Hurdle.

OPPOSITE: An aerial view shows the Leeds and Liverpool Canal bordering the course with the Canal Turn bottom right.

surrounded by the housing estates of Liverpool's north-eastern suburbs, but this all adds to the tag of the National being the 'people's race'.

Pressed by understandable concerns for animal welfare, exacerbated by numerous fatalities over the years, the unique National fences have been gradually altered and suppressed. Even if the drops are not as fearsome and the wooden frames have been replaced by plastic cores, they remain aesthetically similar to how they were and are always dressed with spruce branches, transported by the lorryload from Grizedale Forest in Cumbria.

Thankfully, the result has been a safer race which should provide many more great stories at this unique horse racing venue.

Ascot

Berkshire, England

An elite symbol of pageantry and the royal association with horses, Ascot has been the scene of racing for more than 300 years.

It is known particularly for June's Royal meeting, with carriages containing the reigning monarch and various other regal family members leading a daily procession down the track before the action begins. Spectators in morning dress and extravagant hats watch world-class competition before the communal singing around the bandstand and further merriment among the picnics in the car parks.

The mile-and-three-quarters round course, surrounded by woodland and in a gentle triangular shape, is used throughout the year with jump racing in the winter. It is regarded as essentially wide and fair, but is a little more undulating than it might appear on television. From the far point of the triangle at Swinley Bottom, it rises 73 feet (22 metres) up towards the winning post, a significant climb for a tiring horse.

Fittingly for such a royal institution, it was Queen Anne, who once kept her hounds at Swinley Bottom, who came upon this area of heathland when out riding and in 1711 began a series of races for English Hunters, a stockier breed.

Anne died three years later and royal interest ebbed and flowed. Infrastructure began to appear in the reign of George III with the erection of the Slingsby Stand in 1793. The Gold Cup, Royal Ascot's oldest and signature race, was staged for the first time a few years later. The site was protected as a racecourse for ever more by an Act of Parliament in 1813.

The stark concrete grandstands built in the late 1960s were never particularly loved. They were very modern for the time, even equipped with escalators, but had the air of office blocks and soon began to look dated as time passed.

A £200m redevelopment by architect Populous and main contractor Laing O'Rourke required the track to be closed temporarily and the Royal meeting was held at York in 2005. Many old course artefacts, from signs and iron gates to memorabilia associated with the day in 1996 when Frankie Dettori rode all seven winners, later went to auction.

BELOW: The royal procession passes down the track before racing each afternoon at Royal Ascot.

ABOVE: A victory at Royal Ascot can make a season for both trainer and jockey.

FAR LEFT: There are no fewer than 24 sets of escalators transporting spectators up and down the enormous grandstand.

TOP LEFT: Ascot has long been a place to parade glamorous, extravagant millinery, an association reinforced by the *Ascot Gavotte* in the musical *My Fair Lady* (1964).

LEFT: Queen Elizabeth II attends the presentations for the Gold Cup in June 2017, after James Doyle won on Big Orange.

Ascot was reopened the following year with the expectation that visitors would be greatly impressed by the new 45,000-capacity grandstand with its natural lighting, bowl-shaped parade ring and relaid grass track. This was not universally the case and it caused some ructions among British society, which is often resistant to change.

Those able to promenade along the more upmarket areas towards the top had an unobstructed view but it was felt others in the 'cheap seats' at the bottom had not been accommodated and not everyone could even see the racing. The stand itself, cruelly described in places as resembling a cruise ship or airport terminal, was even thought to have been laid in the wrong place. Royal Enclosure habitués,

that most exclusive club which used to have scrupulous invitation requirements, could not find their old haunts and, perish the thought, even had to mingle with members of the general public at spots on the ground floor.

The famous straight mile, moved 42 metres to the north, had new vagaries and drained far more quickly than the round course. Punters and jockeys alike struggled to understand the effect of the draw.

Douglas Erskine-Crum, the chief executive who had overseen the project and was credited with making Ascot a little more egalitarian during his 13-year tenure, departed. Tweaks here and there by his successor, Charles Barnett, and the next incumbent, Guy Henderson, saw criticism ease, everyone find their place, and for Ascot to retain its status among the world's premier racecourses.

After the royal meeting was extended to five days in 2002 to celebrate the Queen's Golden Jubilee, the closing Saturday has become a huge hit and attempts to attract top-quality international horses have resulted in many winners from America. Black Caviar, the Australian sprinting marvel, was greeted by Queen Elizabeth II after her victory in 2012.

The Shergar Cup, a team jockeys' competition each August, continues to draw a healthy younger audience and the King George VI and Queen Elizabeth Stakes is the mid-season showpiece. The clash between Grundy and Bustino in 1975 is commonly regarded as the greatest race of last century.

In 2011 it was decided that a lucrative new event should be created to bring the curtain down on the European Flat racing season. British Champions Day, the richest Flat meeting in the calendar, could surely only be held in one place.

ABOVE: Coronet (No.5) ridden by Olivier Peslier winning the Ribblesdale Stakes at Royal Ascot in June 2017.

LEFT: Royal Ascot attracts around 300,000 visitors across the five days of racing.

Ashgabat Hippodrome

Turkmenistan

The prevalence of racing in the secretive and little-visited Central Asian country of Turkmenistan owes plenty to its leader, Gurbanguly Berdimuhamedow. The president has an obsession with the Akhal-Teke, an ancient and indigenous breed of horse which is an ancestor of the modern thoroughbred.

The president, who has developed his own personality cult, likes to be known as a sportsman and had the title "National Horse Breeder" bestowed upon him and is depicted in gold aboard one of his horses on a giant marble slab in Ashgabat, the country's capital.

A pedigree Akhal-Teke is a beautiful specimen; straighter, leaner and more finely-boned than a conventional racehorse and graced with a noble head. It evolved to cope with an arid climate and can come in an astonishing spectrum of colours, with a metallic and almost golden sheen. Said to be a favourite of Alexander The Great and Oliver Cromwell, the Akhal-Teke is wilful and intelligent but versatile enough to be used for showing, dressage and show jumping as well as racing.

They were close to extinction in the Soviet era before private breeding was permitted in the 1980s. Geldy Kyarizov has been recognized as a worldwide authority on the horse and its preservation is largely down to him.

He campaigned and researched tirelessly but unfortunately his discovery that, after genetic analysis, the Akhal-Teke blood in many horses at the racecourse had been diluted with thoroughbreds to make them faster led to

his downfall. A supposed denigration of the reputation of Turkmenistan's national symbol led to his imprisonment in 2002 and he later fled to Moscow.

Ashgabat hippodrome is part of an equestrian complex on the eastern outskirts of the eerily quiet city and was constructed by the Turkish firm Etkin at a cost of $100 million. It was opened in 2011 to showcase the Akhal-Teke and is also a breeding and stabling facility.

Visitors are welcomed by a huge portrait of Berdimuhamedow and statues of prancing horses (above right), and will find a smart marble grandstand with gold-coloured seats and a parasol roof. There are views of the Kopet Dag mountains bordering Iran.

They race on Sundays during spring and autumn seasons, clockwise around a wide and easy artificial track. The winners are brought back in by men in colourful national uniform and jockeys receive a carpet, a shawl, or even a car on big days.

Some might have witnessed Berdimuhamedow riding in a race himself at the track in 2013, predictably winning but only to fall off right after the line in a video that, despite state efforts for it to never see the light of day, went viral.

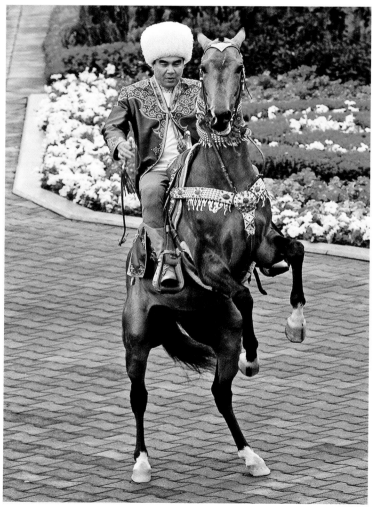

RIGHT: President and consummate horseman Gurbanguly Berdimuhamedow riding the lively winner of the Turkmenistan Annual Horse Beauty Contest.

OPPOSITE: The portrait of the president is only slightly less important than the finishing post.

Baden-Baden

Iffezheim, Germany

There are a great many attractions around the spa town of Baden-Baden from upmarket shopping, to walks in the Black Forest and even skiing in the winter. Back in 1858, Edouard Benazet decided it needed another. The Frenchman, who had inherited Baden-Baden's famous casino from his father Jacques, decided to build a racecourse.

That year the track, just to the north of the town in the village of Iffezheim, hosted a three-day meeting which included the race which remains its most important to this day, the Grosser Preis von Baden. The race proved a more viable concern than the casino, which was shut for decades after the abolition of gambling in Germany in 1872. To safeguard racing at that time, a noble group including princes and counts from Russia and Hungary, as well as the British Duke of Hamilton, ran it under the name of the International Club.

Armed conflicts proved more problematic for Baden-Baden, which was closed during both World Wars, but the Club remained in charge until 2009 when the racecourse had to be saved from the brink of insolvency. It is now run by Baden Racing, chaired by businessman and racehorse owner-breeder Andreas Jacobs.

Thankfully, German racing has emerged from a period in the doldrums and Benazet's creation, close to the banks of the Rhine, remains the jewel in its crown. One of the reasons Baden-Baden is special is that it always leaves punters wanting more. Its meetings are scarce - just a few days

in the spring and autumn and the centrepiece, the so-called Grand Festival Week at the end of August.

The week's highlight is the Grosser Preis von Baden, sponsored by the Swiss watchmaker Longines, which draws plenty of European competition. In the 1870s it was captured three consecutive times by Kincsem, the greatest ever Hungarian horse, and very recently by Danedream, one of only two German animals to have won the Prix de l'Arc de Triomphe at Longchamp.

Although the racing in the Grand Festival is high-class, most of the 20,000 daily attendees go for social reasons. Baden-Baden is the nearest German equivalent to Royal Ascot, if a little more relaxed.

The two main grandstands have terracotta-coloured roofs and are modern in style, offering views of the hills of the Black Forest. There is a gently undulating mile-and-a-quarter grass oval, with a separate six-furlong sprint chute. Inside it are the remains of banks and hedges from an old jumps course. Racing over obstacles used to be popular in Germany but the discipline has now virtually died out.

TOP RIGHT: The stature of the Grosser Preis von Baden is such that the winner is automatically invited to that year's Breeders' Cup Turf.

RIGHT: German-bred horses have been in increasing demand around Europe in recent years.

Royal Bangkok Sports Club

Thailand

Away from the recognizable 'horsey' countries, it is thrilling to discover how many unexpected places have an established racing scene.

Thailand's capital Bangkok has two well-maintained racecourses, which alternate meetings each Sunday, as well as a few regional tracks. The Royal Turf Club, formed in 1961, hosts the biggest race of the calendar, January's Derby Cup. However, the Royal Bangkok Sports Club (RBSC) is the older venue, the sport's headquarters, and is rather more remarkable.

Flanked by hotels of the luxury global chain variety and the bright shopping malls of the Pathum Wan district in the centre of the heaving megalopolis, it is impossible to even guess at how much this green oasis would command were it turned over to property developers.

Luckily, the land has been secured by Royal charter since it was founded in 1901 and is part of Bangkok's most exclusive private members' club. King Rama V had reportedly enjoyed a visit to the races while on a tour of Europe and gave permission for the formation of a course. The first aeroplane ever seen in Thailand took off from the site in 1911.

There can be few more immaculately kept infields of racecourses in the world. The RBSC is home to an 18-hole golf course, a driving range, sports fields and lakes. Those who wish to be admitted and make use of the other facilities, including tennis courts, polo lawn and swimming pool should give up now; many memberships are hereditary and senior executives and politicians pay a rumoured £40,000 to join after waiting years on the list.

However, when opened for racing at weekends, it only costs a couple of pounds, with the seats high up in the stands affording marvellous views of the city and the Skytrain metro system passing along the back straight.

As the track (along with boxing) is one of the only places where betting is legal in Thailand, the clientele has a predictable demographic. Away from the plush members' boxes and restaurants, the facilities are a little rough and ready and the stiff government taxation on betting revenue and the nation's economic crises have made life difficult for the racing side of the business. Nonetheless, a few thousand attend each meeting and the large, two-tiered grandstand is heaving for the King's Cup in February.

Thailand has its own breeding network and the standard of racing and jockeyship around the easy, level turf oval is of a better standard than one might imagine.

Beirut Hippodrome

Lebanon

No racecourse can have been placed in an area with such a tumultuous past, present and future than that of Beirut's, which sits right in the heart of the ancient but damaged city. It has been here since 1916, financed by the Ottoman Turks and built in what was once a large pine forest by a member of one of Lebanon's great families, Alfred Sursock. The hippodrome is one of the oldest in the Middle East and had its glory days between the 1930s and 1960s, with racing twice a week all year, receiving visits from Royal families as far afield as Iran and Greece.

It was restored with great care in the early 1970s by the long-serving general manager Nabil Nasrallah but only in vain, as the outbreak of civil war put the place in a highly compromised position. Beirut racecourse found itself in no-mans land, divided by the line that separated the different Christian and Sunni and Shiite neighbourhoods. Even as the war waged, though, somehow the racing carried on unimpeded.

It was seen as one of the only places residents could mix freely, arriving from separate entrances. "Militia fighters used to shoot at each other all week and meet here on Sunday to place their bets," said trainer, Ali Ahmed Seif, in an interview with the AFP news agency in 2016. It is believed that the various militia would even meet covertly at the track.

Unfortunately, the prominent position of the track meant it could not escape damage. The Israeli air force and tanks destroyed all of the grandstand's columns and the building collapsed in 1982. At one point a ceasefire had to be secured to ensure horses could be removed from the course. It was not until 1990 that a rather less elegant concrete structure was built to replace the classic structure.

The racecourse was not only affected architecturally. Lebanon has a centuries-old association with the Arabian horses that raced there, and many precious bloodlines died out. The numbers in training have dwindled into the hundreds rather than thousands and the venue is run by the Society for the Protection and Improvement of the Arabian Horse in Lebanon (SPARCA).

Meetings now take place once a week on a seven-furlong, red sand oval, which is overlooked by tower blocks along with the smart French embassy, installed in a building which Sursock intended to be used as a casino. A few fine Lebanon cedars remain in the middle. Events can attract a healthy and excitable crowd, sitting on plastic chairs or standing on the dilapidated steps. Horses are saddled outside and the weighing room does not look as if it would pass many health and safety tests.

The chief concern now is that the racecourse is one of the few green spaces left in central Beirut. SPARCA wants to find common ground and believes that investment in reviving the racing scene would provide a genuine economic opportunity, as well as preserving a piece of local history. Others in power would like to turn it into a park and golf course, while the threat of the developers' diggers lurks in the background.

TOP: The old stabling from the early twentieth century has been encircled by modern development.

ABOVE: A 'Then and Now' comparison of the old hippodrome and the new grandstand rebuilt after the Israeli occupation.

Belmont Park

New York, America

Belmont Park is the home of the Belmont Stakes, the final leg of what is now known as the American Triple Crown. But it has not been ever thus.

In fact, not only is the race almost 40 years older than the racecourse, it predates the other Triple Crown races, the Kentucky Derby and Preakness, by eight years and six respectively.

Belmont Park was built in 1905 for the eye-watering sum of $2.5 million, by former Secretary of the Navy, William Collins Whitney and August Belmont II. The latter's German-born father, of the same name, founded a banking empire and his great contribution to the American racing industry had prompted the Belmont Stakes to be named after him. The race was first staged in 1867 at Jerome Park, New York, and later Morris Park.

Both venues had closed by the time Belmont, on the border with Queens on Long Island, had opened to a crowd of 40,000. It was not plain sailing; all tracks in New York closed between 1911 and 1912 because of restrictive gambling legislation and there was a suspicious fire in 1917 that caused great damage.

By 1963, Belmont had to lock its doors again for six years as the grandstands had severe structural issues and were demolished.

A replacement was designed by arguably America's greatest architect, Frank Lloyd Wright. The great innovator created a venue in a radical, medieval style, complete with a roof designed to look like a tent. However, it was rejected for being too non-conformist by the committee and Arthur Froelich's plan, similar to the brick and sandstone buildings that had gone before, was chosen. The stands, which are 1266 ft (386m) long, are not unattractive but surely Lloyd Wright's idea would have given them more distinction.

Froelich also preserved the paddock, which has railings taken from the old Jerome Park. A tree in the middle, known as the White Pine, is thought to be around 200 years old and forms part of Belmont's logo.

What is known as the Triple Crown today was not a commonly accepted achievement when Sir Barton became the first horse to complete wins in all three American classics in 1919. In those days there were other long-forgotten races to be won. It was only after Gallant Fox became the second horse to collect the triple in 1930 that the phrase was coined. The series then became the *de facto* programme for the best three-year-old colts.

Even so, scheduling suitable space for recovery between the Derby, on the first Saturday in May,

the Preakness a fortnight later, and the Belmont three weeks after that, was not formalized until 1969.

Belmont Park is known as 'Big Sandy', because its mile-and-a-half dirt circuit is the longest in America. As the Belmont Stakes is over a full lap, a longer distance than a three-year-old colt will have attempted before, it is known as the 'Test of the Champion' and it has proved a bridge too far for many over the years. The racecourse is on a grand scale, with 430 acres (174 hectares) including training facilities on some valuable

New York real estate. A record crowd of 120,000 crammed in to see Smarty Jones get caught by outsider Birdstone in 2004 when attempting to secure a first Triple Crown since Affirmed in 1978. Belmont, which also has a Turf course inside the dirt, has quite a busy programme from May through to July, takes a break during the August meeting at Saratoga, and returns for an autumn season. It has other important events besides the Belmont Stakes, and many of the sport's biggest stars from Man O'War to Citation, Kelso, Cigar and Curlin, have returned in October for the Jockey Club Gold Cup.

ABOVE: Horses and riders head to the course from Belmont's long-established parade ring.

TOP RIGHT: The start of the 2017 Belmont Stakes, run in fine June weather.

RIGHT AND FAR RIGHT: Tapwrit, ridden by Jose Ortiz, wins the 149th Belmont Stakes in June 2017.

Birdsville

Queensland, Australia

For two days every September, a one-horse town miles from anywhere becomes a several hundred horse town overrun by many more revellers. Birdsville, in the heart of the outback and close to the border between Queensland and South Australia, supports just over 100 residents and its racecourse was formed shortly after the first European prospectors arrived in the late nineteenth century.

The track is in a claypan, or shallow depression, in the red dunes of the desert and supports 13 low-quality contests around a mile-and-a-quarter circuit with a five-furlong sprint chute. It is one of only a handful of tracks in the state to race anti-clockwise and the feature one-mile Birdsville Cup is one of the oldest races in the country.

However, visitors are not really there for any serious form study and it has grown into a carnival rather different to when it began in 1882.

The Queenslander newspaper described the first meeting as being "largely attended, nearly 160 station owners, managers, stockmen, and other employees being present". It added that: "The settling took place in Mr. Tucker's hotel, where the amounts were paid over to the respective

RIGHT: In 2016 Layla Cross made Birdsville history by riding Moore Alpha to victory in the Birdsville Cup race. It was the first time in the race's 134-year history that a female jockey and trainer combination had won.

BELOW: Ladies Day at Birdsville is a far more casual affair than those at Goodwood or Royal Ascot.

winners, the usual toasts proposed and duly responded to, after which a meeting was held in Messrs. Burt and Co's large iron store, when a jockey club was formed."

Due to its far-flung location, Birdsville has become a cult event on the Australian calendar, drawing the hardest of hardcore travellers in much the same way as the Burning Man music festival in Nevada.

Not everyone comes for the racing but 8,000 partake in sideshows including Fred Brophy's notorious and long-running boxing tent, various forms of gambling and a considerable amount of drinking. The only watering hole, the Birdsville Hotel, quickly finds itself surrounded by a moat of discarded beer cans. It is all largely well-behaved and raises valuable funds for the Royal Flying Doctor Service.

The tiny airport is jammed full of light aircraft and even the horses have travelled from other states to take on the local bush enthusiasts, joining the human campers for a few days in temporary accommodation.

Despite being on the edge of the Simpson Desert, racing was delayed for a day for the first time anyone could remember in 2016 after a third of the annual rainfall fell in just a few hours and left the area cut off.

ABOVE RIGHT: Furlong markers are more rudimentary than those at Flemington and Randwick.

RIGHT: Sometimes known as the Birdsville Race Carnival, up to 6,000 spectators are expected at the annual event, held each September.

OPPOSITE: After torrential rain in 2016 racing was suspended for a day to allow the flooded course to drain. The Birdsville Cup was run the next day under clear blue skies.

Hippodrome de Borely

Marseille, France

Borely is one of Marseille's two urban racecourses but it is a far more substantial proposition than the all-weather facility at Pont-de-Vivaux out towards the east of the city.

It is only seen in its full glory from above, revealing the spectacular setting right on the coast, with the vibrant green of the track standing out against the azure of the Mediterranean.

There have been meetings here since 1860, held in the grounds of the Château Borely (to the right of the racetrack in the aerial photo). The fine house was built by the family which bears its name, a local mercantile dynasty, in the eighteenth century and it was given to the city in the nineteenth. It is very French in style, filled with frescoes and *trompe l'oeil*, and is now home to museums of earthenware and decorative arts. In the grounds, before reaching the boundary of the racecourse, are formal English, French and Japanese gardens.

The château itself can be seen on the back straight from ground level, along with the gardens and some far more modern and

rather less attractive hotel and residential developments.

Racing in France is decidedly Paris-centric but there have been moves by the racing authority France-Galop to ensure that some of the principal midweek meetings are staged at provincial tracks, so they gain a slice of the national betting proceeds.

Borely is one of the recipients and has a few days during the year which draw the top jockeys and the better horses down from the capital. There are a few Listed level races and the Grand Prix de Marseille in the autumn is a handicap worth at least €52,000.

Jump racing takes place on many cards through the year, too, using the same grass one-mile oval circuit. Inside is a trotting track, which was added to Borely's portfolio in 1999.

Závodiska Bratislava

Bratislava, Slovakia

If an unwitting racegoer were teleported straight into the grandstands of Bratislava's racecourse, they would probably believe they had arrived at a particularly rural venue somewhere in Central Europe as they looked over the 28 hectares (69 acres) of tree-lined parkland.

It betrays very little of its location, right in the middle of the largest housing estate on the continent. With 120,000 residents, Petrzalka is the most populated district in Bratislava, and was constructed in 1973 when it was part of the former Czechoslovakia. The area is not unsafe but certainly has a menacing look to it with row after row of pre-fab high-rise blocks known as 'panelaks' to the locals.

There is a long and proud history of horse racing and breeding in Slovakia with anecdotal evidence of meetings taking place long before a formal association was drawn up in 1840. There have been races held in Bratislava since 1868, close to the present course in what is now known as Sad Janka Krala, a park on the southern bank of the Danube which features some interesting Gothic towers.

When the country was part of the Austro-Hungarian Empire, Bratislava briefly hosted a national equivalent of the 2000 Guineas, a race which was later moved to Vienna.

Nowadays it holds the full pack of five Classic races, which are scheduled to fit in with those in the Czech Republic, so that the Slovak Derby winner can then represent the nation in the Czech version.

There are usually around 15 meetings at Bratislava, including Flat and jump racing, with half a dozen more fixtures dotted around a few provincial locations. Visitors can expect to see a good standard of competition and often runners from the Czech Republic and occasionally even further afield. It received publicity on the day of the Slovak Derby in 2010, but not for that particular race. The sprinter Overdose, considered the second best Hungarian horse in history after the well-travelled mare Kincsem in the 1870s, reappeared after a 15-month injury layoff to win for the 13th consecutive time in a minor event on the Derby undercard.

Organisers have tried to build up the profile of the Slovak Derby, usually held in mid-July, by flying in international jockeys. In 1993 it was won by the great jockey Lester Piggott aboard Zimzalabim, trained in England by Barry Hills, and in 2002 the top prize was taken by Frankie Dettori and the German-trained horse Muskatsturm.

TOP: Major races in Bratislava can attract runners from across Central and Eastern Europe.

ABOVE: Some of the fences on the steeplechase course have a fearsome reputation.

Cartmel

Cumbria, England

Gridlock on the Lake District's roads over a summer weekend is not always caused by those wanting a walk around Windermere or to discover Beatrix Potter country. Thousands are attempting to navigate the winding lanes in time to get a picnic spot at Cartmel.

The meetings the course holds are all over Bank Holidays, and their scarcity makes them all the more special. Set in a pristine, rambling landscape of hills, fields and dry stone walls as part of the Holker Estate, it is informal racing at its very best.

It is believed that Cartmel has been a recognized track since 1856 but its executive is sure that unlicensed racing had taken place from centuries earlier. Being so remote, Cartmel took the shape of a glorified point-to-point with local amateur jockeys involved for many years.

A lot of this changed in the 1960s under chairman Colonel Davy Pain and Tim Riley, the clerk of the course and managing director. Sponsorship was introduced, along with a fairground, and it became something of a tourist attraction for thousands. Hugh Cavendish, the Baron of Furness, has been a benevolent and guiding landowner. The leading-name jockeys

will travel up if not required elsewhere and there are frequent runners across from Ireland.

The racecourse stages only jump racing, and is constrained in a curious shape. A tight oval of around nine furlongs bisects itself and the half-mile run-in after the final obstacle on the steeplechase course is the longest in the country. It is not possible to see the horses at every point and the races are of a very modest level. No-one seems to care, as Cartmel is not trying to be Royal Ascot. Anyone involved in owning or training a winning horse receives one of the famous sticky toffee puddings from the nearby Village Shop.

Perhaps the most memorable incident to have happened on the racecourse itself is now part of gambling mythology. Back in 1974, a group of Irishmen nearly pulled off the most audacious of coups by using a ringer. They sent a chestnut

LEFT: The field makes its way down the back straight during the Station Yard Garage Handicap in August 2017.

TOP AND MIDDLE RIGHT: Though many of the fences look like they could lead into someone's garden, this particular hurdle is a bit of racecourse dressing, as evidenced from the photo below it.

BOTTOM RIGHT: Still everything to play for in the Hadwins Motor Group Handicap Hurdle.

horse registered by the name Gay Future which was actually a fairly useless animal called Arctic Chevalier to Tony Collins, a well-heeled but less than prolific trainer in Scotland, and told him to enter it for Cartmel. Meanwhile, the real Gay Future was being readied in Ireland by the skilled Edward O'Grady. They switched the horses in a lay-by and when he was being saddled up, covered Gay Future in soapflakes to look as if he was sweating unfavourably.

Bets had been placed in multiples all over London, tied up with a couple of decoys to throw the bookmakers off the scent. The jockey was a late switch from an unknown to the capable amateur Tim Jones who tried to look like he didn't know what he was doing when mounting in the paddock. The gang had taken many other precautions to prevent word getting out and Gay Future won easily at 10-1.

The root of the deception was later discovered by a journalist and Collins was one of two men found guilty of conspiracy to defraud.

He returned, unrepentant, to the course at the recent 40-year anniversary of an event which still captures the imagination.

LEFT: With only a small grandstand, vantage points are taken all over the winding racecourse.

BELOW: With staggeringly beautiful scenery it's not surprising that crowds can reach 20,000. A three-day meeting takes five days, with a day in between racing days to clear up.

BOTTOM: Runners measure up a fence on the immaculately prepared course.

Champ de Mars

Mauritius

It is impressive that the remote Indian Ocean island of Mauritius, a country smaller than Luxembourg, has a racecourse at all, let alone one with such tradition and framework.

Champ de Mars is believed to be the oldest active racecourse in the southern hemisphere and is home to a thriving scene in the capital St Louis. The city is hemmed in by the imposing Moka mountain range and these volcanic remnants make for a splendid backdrop to the track.

The first meeting, in 1812, came just after Britain had seized control of Mauritius from France and it was hoped the sport would foster some congeniality between the existing and arriving administration.

Along with the governor, Sir Robert Farquhar, the driving force behind Champ de Mars in its early days was Colonel Edward Draper, who would regularly ride his horse, Restoration, in races. Draper was a somewhat controversial figure who opposed the abolition of slavery, but he is still remembered as the founder of Mauritian racing and events run over 1500 metres are still held over what is known as 'The Draper's Mile'.

Racing successfully reunited this cultural melting pot and it essentially became the national sport, with wide-ranging media coverage and a number of dedicated publications each week.

There are meetings most Saturdays from March onwards and they always attract large and boisterous crowds. The turf track looks largely unchanged from the early descriptions. The oval circuit of just over six furlongs is so narrow, at around 13 metres (43 feet), that a maximum of 11 horses can compete.

Narrow grandstands, last updated in the 1950s, are a little ramshackle and in need of an update, but this might detract from the intimate atmosphere. They are separated from the track by a road that is closed during meetings and when horses are exercising in the early mornings, but is re-opened for the school run at 7.30am. The paddock and winner's enclosure behind them are particularly pretty.

A breeding industry has never been instigated so horses have always had to be imported. There are around 400 in training, half of which are trained at the racecourse, and the majority of them come from South Africa. The year's most prestigious race is the Maiden Cup, held over a mile and a half each September. A record attendance of over 100,000 watched the 1984 edition.

Chantilly

Oise, France

If Goodwood provides the quintessentially English racing occasion, so one could be nowhere but France when visiting Chantilly.

Catching the eye from the ornate grandstand is the stunning building of the Grandes Ecuries, or Great Stables, which lines almost a furlong of the back straight. It was commissioned by Louis Henri, the Duc de Bourbon, to house 240 horses and more than 500 hounds. Jean Aubert's architectural masterpiece is now an equine museum.

Those entering the course by road will already have seen the Château de Chantilly itself, which stands around the corner from the stables. A site of an ancestral home since the Middle Ages, but rebuilt on several occasions, it was used as a prison during the French Revolution and the main wing was destroyed in 1799. The present Renaissance incarnation, completed for the Henri d'Orleans in 1882, sits by a lake and is filled with the largest collection of Old Masters outside the Louvre gallery and an extraordinary collection of wooden and gilded furniture.

ABOVE: The Château de Chantilly with the racecourse stretching out beyond. It is a fitting backdrop to France's most beautiful racecourse.

RIGHT: Horses race past Les Grandes Ecuries. The former stables had fallen into disrepair until renovated in the 1980s, and reopened as the Living Museum of the Horse.

Racing, unsurprisingly, followed on from the aristocratic pursuit of hunting in the nearby forest. In 1833, Prince Lobanoff emerged onto the Orleans family's vast lawn on his horse and decided to race his friends to the Ecuries.

A meeting was established the next year and wooden viewing platforms sprang up, later replaced by grandstands designed by Honore Daumet, who also worked on the château. Mercifully, his stylish stone structures remain to this day.

The right-handed circuit, with several interlocking courses, now has the addition of an all-weather surface. Situated about 40 kilometres (25 miles) north of Paris, it is not as obviously accessible or as popular as city-centre Longchamp but the racing is of equivalent quality. The most important event in its schedule ought to be the Prix du Jockey Club (French Derby). However, the subsequent Prix de Diane (French Oaks) fixture attracts the bigger crowd and has the atmosphere of a sophisticated picnic.

As well as being more commonly known for its cream and lace, Chantilly is also home to a couple of thousand of France's best racehorses. Wooded gallops to the south of the racecourse open out into a huge expanse of open grassland, Les Aigles. André Fabre, the perennial French champion trainer, is among the residents along with the members of the great Head dynasty, Alec, Freddy and Criquette.

There is an academy, and, less pleasantly, a dedicated hospital for jockeys in this centre of French racing. There is also a polo lawn and an international standard show jumping course, making it a stop on the show jumping world tour.

A few different parts of Chantilly were used in *A View To A Kill*, with Roger Moore's James Bond visiting the Château and later riding against the villain Max Zorin over a booby-trapped jumps course. But despite the scenery and the impossible charm of the place, harking back to a glamorous bygone era, the recent history was not at all rosy.

In the mid-1990s, the French racing industry was subsiding from low attendances and the associated financial turnover and it was decided that one Parisian racecourse would be closed. Chantilly, at that point looking a little tatty, was chosen and it was only saved by a last-minute intervention from investors including the francophile Aga Khan, spiritual leader of the Ismaeli muslims. With a world-renowned breeding empire a couple of miles outside the town as well as dozens of his horses stabled within it, the Aga Khan has also continued to support the racecourse. The grandstands retained their original style but were spruced up, and new restaurant, hospitality boxes and a paddock complex were created.

LEFT: Brametot (near side) comes with a well-timed run to win the 2017 Prix du Jockey Club (French Derby), the track's most significant race of the year.

BELOW: Situated 40 kilometres from the centre of Paris, Chantilly has never been as popular as its suburban rival, Longchamp.

RIGHT: Stephane Pasquier riding Senga wins the Prix de Diane Longines at Chantilly, June 18, 2017.

Cheltenham

Gloucestershire, England

There is an intoxicating atmosphere about Cheltenham racecourse which draws so many thousands back year after year.

It is often described as a natural amphitheatre, guarded by the rolling Cotswold hills and the sharp limestone escarpment of Cleeve Hill. For the four days in March of the Cheltenham Festival, the amphitheatre becomes a cauldron.

Cheltenham is the spiritual and physical home of British jump racing, heralding the start of the serious season at November's Open meeting, and later the highlights of the winter's endeavour at the Festival with its series of championship events.

Enthusiasts descend en-masse from Ireland and across the country for the Festival packing out hotels as far away as Malvern in Worcestershire. Following weeks of build-up in the media, trial races on the track and a host of preview panels, there is a lusty roar as the tape is raised for the opening race on the Tuesday, the Supreme Novices' Hurdle.

A prodigious amount of betting and Guinness-drinking takes place within this sea of tweed and Barbour jackets, with 70,000 attending Friday's Cheltenham Gold Cup.

Such frivolity has not always been allowed to pass uninterrupted. Flat race meetings in the early nineteenth century were held on Cleeve Hill and were fiercely opposed by the abstemious local Anglican reverend, Francis Close.

He would preach and organize protests against the evils of gambling and it is said that rocks and bottles were thrown at the runners and riders in 1829. A year later there was an incident of arson at the course and it was moved to its now-permanent home at nearby Prestbury Park.

Jumping did not begin there until 1898, when that moved from nearby Andoversford, and some of the Cheltenham Festival's venerable prizes, such as the Grand Annual and National Hunt Chase, predate the modern racecourse. The Cheltenham Gold Cup, the most coveted prize in the sport alongside the Grand National, was not staged over fences until 1924.

The track, stretched out around the 350 acres (142 hectares), can appear complicated to newcomers. It consists of two interlocking loops of steeplechases and hurdles; the Old Course and New Course, which alternate in use through the season. In the middle is the weaving Cross Country Course, full of banks, rails, brushes and ditches. It was built in 1985 to replicate similar

ABOVE: Robbie Power on Sizing John is cheered back to the winners' enclosure after winning the Gold Cup on the final day of the 2017 Cheltenham Festival.

RIGHT: The unmistakeable colours of Rich Ricci worn by Ruby Walsh leading on Vroum Vroum Mag in the OLBG Mares' Hurdle at the 2016 Festival.

RIGHT: Around 265,000 pints of Guinness are consumed during the Festival, along with 120,000 bottles of wine and 20,000 bottles of the house champagne.

FAR RIGHT: The parade ring as viewed at the 2015 Festival.

BELOW: The Old and New Courses are used at different meetings through the year and run alongside each other at certain places. They are well marked out with rails and posts to avoid confusion for jockeys.

races in France and Ireland and to encourage European competition. Cheltenham is a demanding track with a tricky descent, providing a test for even the best jumpers and the finish, which is an uphill climb, is a nasty surprise for a tiring horse.

It is a place where equine heroes are made, including the only five-time Gold Cup winner Golden Miller back in the 1930s. Arkle, considered the greatest steeplechaser of all time, raced there five times and won the first of three consecutive Gold Cups in 1964 after a much-publicized duel with Mill House.

Both horses have popular bars named after them in the main grandstand while names like Dawn Run, Desert Orchid, Istabraq and Kauto Star have etched their names into folklore with their exploits over the years. A recent moment to savour came in 2016 when the dashing Sprinter Sacre, feared to be a spent force after suffering from an irregular heartbeat, regained his Queen Mother Champion Chase title.

Something more akin to the present-day Cheltenham Festival began to take shape in the 1960s as the crowds increased. New stands were built and an enclosure created in the centre of the course. The main grandstand, with five floors and a panoramic restaurant, was finished by the 1980s.

It remains the jewel in the crown of the Jockey Club Racecourse group and there was a mixture of excitement and apprehension when a belated £45 million redevelopment was completed, on budget and on time, in 2015.

The Queen Mother Stand, an outmoded building housing long-serving box-holders, was removed and replaced by the Princess Royal Stand. The new structure, by developers Kier, and architects Roberts Limbrick, met with almost unanimous approval. It is of an amber stone colour, tastefully in keeping with the Cotswold landscape, and offers the lucky few as luxurious an entertainment facility as can be found in sport. Also unveiled was a crescent walkway, wrapping all the way around to the paddock, to increase viewing.

BELOW LEFT: The Princess Royal Stand (on the right) has made the view looking towards the finish more impressive since it was finished in 2015.

BELOW: The economic turnover of the Cheltenham Festival for Gloucestershire is said to be in excess of £100 million.

BOTTOM: Harper Adams University students pose in front of the statue of the 1966 Gold Cup winner, Arkle, illuminated in green for St. Patrick's Day.

Chester

Cheshire, England

Chester would be a remarkable enough racecourse for its setting alone. Furthermore, it is believed to be the oldest working track in Britain and quite possibly the world. There have been meetings on the banks of the River Dee from 1539, when it was used to provide some alternative civic entertainment to the brutal annual Shrove Tuesday football match.

Racing has been staged virtually ever since then and Chester Racecourse is often referred to as 'The Roodee'. This roughly translates as the 'island of the cross' because in Saxon times the land was covered by the Dee apart from a small raised mound bearing a stone cross, or 'Rood'. It was Chester's harbour, where ships unloaded.

It is the sport's gain that the river gradually silted up, and the track has been roughly the same shape since the 1730s. An incredibly tight circuit of only a mile round, sandwiched between the city walls, the river and a railway viaduct, it offers a huge advantage to horses drawn towards the inside rail.

It becomes the focus of the British racing world, as well as the Cheshire social scene, for the three midweek days of the May meeting. The Chester Cup, originally called the Tradesmen's Cup, is a fiercely competitive handicap over two and a quarter miles and the main event of the festival.

The 1844 renewal of the Cup resulted in one of the great betting coups in history when Red Deer, ridden by Sam Kitchener under a minuscule weight of 4st, landed bets worth £100,000 for owner Lord George Bentinck. It is said that no stone was left unturned in making sure Red Deer won, including greasing the palm of the rival jockey of the well-fancied former winner Alice Hawthorn, who was carrying 5.5st more in any case. Helpfully for Bentinck, a renowned gambler, he was also the race starter and could ensure Red Deer was in the right position.

Races like the Chester Vase, Dee Stakes and Cheshire Oaks are other long-established pointers for the rest of the season, even if the horse racing matters little to many of the visitors before they spill out for what is the briefest of strolls towards the bright lights of the ancient city.

Chester Racecourse is a limited company which also encompasses nearby Bangor-on-Dee and has benefited from strong, go-ahead management. It has gradually become an aspirational venue for the affluent north-west set and attracts enormous crowds even for mundane weekend and evening meetings throughout the summer. Parking, though, remains famously difficult to find.

Space being at a premium, the paddock and entertainment marquees are in the centre of the course. It was a familiar sight even after the turn of this century to see horses being walked through the streets of the city to race, until land was acquired to build more practical stabling nearby. The Tattersalls, County and Dee stands offer a fine sight of the winning post but curiously the best view of all can be gained for free, standing on the adjacent ancient city walls.

ABOVE: The racecourse played host to Buffalo Bill's Wild West Show in 1903, but it now stages polo events and, like many racecourses in Britain and Ireland, music festivals.

Churchill Downs

Kentucky, America

The twin hexagonal spires atop the Churchill Downs grandstand have become the symbol of the home of the American horse industry, and its most famous race in particular.

Surprisingly, the spires were only a late addition to the drawings of young Joseph Dominic Baldez as he worked on the designs in 1895, looking for something to make the building stand out a little more. To this day, rarely does a picture of the Kentucky Derby fail to include them.

The Derby and Churchill Downs itself had been going for 20 years before Valdez's input. Several other tracks had been closed down in the Kentucky area but Colonel Meriwether Lewis Clark Jr. was not deterred from his project. Back from a trip to Europe, where he watched the Derby at Epsom and met significant officials from the French and British scene, he had grand ideas of revolutionizing betting and creating a showcase arena for the state.

Clark leased land from a couple of uncles and sold memberships in advance to raise $32,000 to fund construction. Aristides won his first Kentucky Derby in 1875 and it was soon to become the premier event for three-year-old colts. Nevertheless, it still took some years for Churchill Downs to become a financially viable concern and it was taken over by a syndicate of businessmen, headed by the mayor of Louisville Charles Grainger, at the turn of the twentieth century.

Horses began to run in the Derby over a mile and a quarter and then go on to compete in the Preakness Stakes at Pimlico and the Belmont Stakes in New York. The pursuit of the Triple Crown is the only racing event which captures the attention of the wider U.S. public, heightened by the fact that in 2015 American Pharoah became the first to complete it for 37 years.

There are two seasons of meetings, in the spring and autumn, and the Derby arrives promptly on the first Saturday in May. The top-rate spot is in the grandstand, with the infield more resembling an open-air music festival with tales of high spirits and debauchery. Most will not see a horse at all, let alone any of the race described as 'the most exciting two minutes in sports'.

It is still a day of traditions, with a signature sweet bourbon cocktail called the mint julep and the rousing singing of *My Old Kentucky Home* as the horses make their way to the stalls. The winning horse is given a garland of 400 red roses.

Churchill Downs is to the south of Louisville, a city on the banks of the Ohio River which has undergone something of a cultural renaissance. The racecourse, conventional oval with a turf course, does not have the most impressive of suburban backdrops but is important enough to have its own museum with two floors of interactive exhibitions, silks, trophies and even a real, four-legged resident.

Louisville is also on the doorstep of Kentucky's Bluegrass Region. The lush terrain lends itself to raising horses and it has become America's premier breeding centre, with 450 farms dotted around the area. Coolmore, Three Chimneys and Lane's End are swanky examples, while a few former Derby winners, like the striking Silver Charm, have wound down at the Old Friends retirement centre.

TOP AND ABOVE: After persistent rain for several days beforehand, conditions for the 2017 Kentucky Derby were described as "Wet Fast". The crowd still numbered 158,000.

OPPOSITE: Always Dreaming ridden by John Velazquez passes the famous twin spires en route to winning the 143rd Kentucky Derby.

The Curragh

Kildare, Ireland

The vast, glacially-formed plain of the Curragh features deeply in Irish mythology and the tales of Finn MacCool. Legend has it that in the fifth century Saint Brigid, the miracle-working nun, asked the King of Leinster for a piece of land that her cloak would cover in return for making his large ears smaller. When both requests were granted, she spread her cloak wide enough to cover the whole of the Curragh, which is still referred to as St. Brigid's Pastures.

There has been hunting in the area for hundreds of years, which segued into informal race meetings for the aristocracy in the seventeenth century. The first recorded meeting was in 1727, and many present-day regulars might joke that facilities have not improved much since then.

Fluctuations in the Irish economy have caused the redevelopment of the Curragh to stall but finally the wrecking ball was aimed at the shabby, dark grandstands at the start of 2017, to make way for a sparkling new one. Stretching for nearly 5,000 acres, it is regarded as one of the oldest semi-natural grasslands in Europe.

There is no hiding place for a horse on the track itself. A wide, right-handed horseshoe with one gentle bend, it can accommodate Flat racing at distances up to two miles. It is the home of the majority of domestic Group 1 races and all five Classics; the 1,000 and 2,000 Guineas on a weekend at the end of May, the Derby at the end of June, the Oaks in mid-July and the St Leger in early September.

Tipperary-based Aidan O'Brien has had most of these prizes in almost constant possession over the last two decades and brings through his next generation of stars in the autumn two-year-old deciders, the National Stakes and the Moyglare Stud Stakes.

The Irish Derby, first staged in 1866, has long been the next natural target for the winner of the Epsom edition. One of those to complete the double was Shergar, following up his record-breaking 10-length win in Britain by coming home clear under Lester Piggott in little more than a canter in 1981.

The Aga Khan's colt was to be involved in an even more newsworthy incident at the Curragh less than two years later. About to embark upon his second breeding season at Ballymany Stud, only a mile away from the racecourse, Shergar was snatched as part of what has long been assumed to have been an Irish Republican Army kidnapping, and was never seen again.

Irish racegoers are, as a rule, keener on the winter jumps racing and Derby Day, by some way the Curragh's biggest social event, is of far greater value to the professional community through the unimpaired quality of the surface and the position of its races in the calendar. The area is also home to the sport's governing body, the Irish Turf Club.

Around a quarter of Irish horses are trained on the Curragh and there are many miles of grass,

peat, sand, wood-chip and artificial gallops as well as schooling grounds for jumpers. Decorated trainers like Dermot Weld and John Oxx occupy the grander properties while there are many other smaller operations dotted down side roads. Early each morning, the Curragh is a hive of activity as horses arrive from different directions to exercise.

ABOVE: Jockey coach Warren O'Connor walks the course with jockeys Ellen Hennessy, Robbie Dolan and Conor McGovern while his daughters enjoy the firm going for cartwheels.

RIGHT: Donnacha O'Brien on Happily (right) edges out Ryan Moore on Magical to win the Moyglare Stud Stakes during the Longines Irish Champions Weekend in September, 2017.

Del Mar

California, America

Del Mar has epitomized old-school Hollywood cool since its opening day in 1937, when Bing Crosby himself was manning the ticket gates. The great crooner had decided to invest in building a new racecourse with other theatrical accomplices, like Pat O'Brien and Oliver Hardy. The legalization of on-course betting had seen the Californian industry booming and Crosby, who also lived in San Diego County, was persuaded to get involved.

Stands, weighing rooms and stables were built in a Spanish Revival style with a lavish clubhouse for the glitterati. It caused such interest that 15,000 came for the opening meeting and, being just a stone's throw from the Pacific Ocean, it soon became a hot summer destination.

The racetrack drew idols of the movie scene in Los Angeles, such as W. C. Fields, Mickey Rooney, Ava Gardner and Betty Grable; many choosing to make a few days of it by staying in beachfront apartments. The parties would begin on the train from Union Station down to, as Crosby sang, "Where the Turf Meets the Surf".

The racing got off to a strong start, too, with the mighty Seabiscuit defeating Lingaroti in a match race in 1938. There was a very different duel in

2011 when Mike Smith and Chantal Sutherland took their tempestuous relationship onto the track in the so-called 'Battle of the Exes'.

Del Mar is leased from the state and its summer racing season usually runs for a few weeks from July. It has only been interrupted by World War II, when the facility was used to train U.S. Marines.

A bigger and better grandstand was added in 1993, much in keeping with the original style. A mile dirt oval surrounds a tighter grass track, enclosing palm trees and a couple of lakes.

Apart from the July meeting the grounds are used for horse shows and the San Diego County Fair. The nationwide struggle to persuade Americans to go racing does not seem to apply to Del Mar. It might no longer be the preferred destination of the Hollywood set but the management have succeeded in making it appeal to younger people, and women in particular. It earned the right to host the 2017 Breeders' Cup championships and some 45,000 still flock to the opening day, where everyone wears a hat.

The Pacific Classic, a richly-endowed dirt race over a mile and a quarter, is regarded as the

annual highlight each August and in 1996 was the scene of an unexpected defeat for Cigar, who was attempting to better the record of 16 consecutive wins set by Citation in 1950. Zenyatta, who made it to 19 in a row with her crowd-pleasing last-to-first style, won Del Mar's Clement L. Hirsch Stakes three times between 2008 and 2010.

ABOVE: Collected, ridden by Martin Garcia, holds off the charge of Arrogate in the TVG Pacific Classic in front of the Del Mar grandstand.

OPPOSITE: Arrogate, with jockey Mike Smith, before the running of the Pacific Classic in August, 2017.

Doncaster

Yorkshire, England

Doncaster's most famous race has been run in countries far and wide as well as maintaining a strong link with the South Yorkshire market town.

The St Leger is the world's oldest Classic race, first held four years before the Derby in 1776. It was a race for three-year-olds over two miles devised by Major General Anthony St Leger, a member of parliament and renowned local breeder. Its first two runnings were on Cantley Common, an area to the east of Doncaster, before being moved to its present location in 1778 on what is still often known as Town Moor.

Newmarket established the 2000 Guineas in the nineteenth century and the formula evolved for the best colts to be tested over a mile in the Guineas, a mile and a half in the Derby and cap it off over what was later shortened to a mile and three-quarters in the St Leger. West Australian was the first to achieve this Triple Crown in 1853 and Nijinsky the fifteenth and most recent in 1970.

The pattern has been copied worldwide, although sometimes using different race titles, and there are St Legers as far afield as Australia, Switzerland, Jamaica and Poland.

Fillies regularly run against the colts here, with Oh So Sharp achieving a rare female Triple Crown by adding the Leger to her victories in the 1000 Guineas and Oaks.

The race has not been held exclusively at Doncaster, and has had temporary homes at Newmarket and York, Thirsk and even Manchester during wartime. When it returned home to Doncaster crowds were said to reach 300,000.

If there is a true test of stamina for a thoroughbred, it is here. A flat and wide, pear-shaped track of nearly two miles is deceptively demanding and the Leger is usually on softer ground than horses will have encountered due to its autumnal position in the calendar. Many will begin to struggle on the four-and-a-half-furlong home straight.

There are also some fine and curious traditions. The winning jockey receives a (usually greatly outsized) cap to wear and the first baby born

LEFT: Silvestre de Sousa riding Desert Skyline wins the Doncaster Cup Stakes at the 2017 William Hill St Leger Festival.

Epsom

Surrey, England

It was not long after Henry Wicker discovered by accident the restorative qualities of Epsom salts in the Surrey countryside early in the seventeenth century that the area began receiving health-conscious visitors from far and wide.

Racing soon became an additional attraction and under the patronage of Charles II, the first recorded meeting took place in 1661. A century or so later, the race that spawned myriad imitations was first devised. The 12th Earl of Derby and Sir Charles Bunbury, both renowned owners of the time, tossed a coin as to the name of a new race for the best three-year-old colts. The winner barely needs revealing. The equivalent event for fillies would be named The Oaks after the name of Derby's house nearby.

Bunbury at least had the compensation of winning the inaugural Derby in 1780 with his horse Diomed and the race quickly gained in importance and started to attract thousands of spectators.

Master breeder Federico Tesio, the honorary father of racing in Italy, has a memorable quote. "The thoroughbred exists because its selection has depended, not on experts, technicians, or zoologists, but on a piece of wood: the winning post of the Epsom Derby."

Quite why this became the case still appears bizarre to this day. Epsom seems so unsuitable as a setting of such singular importance. The horseshoe-shaped track on the North Downs has such cambers that it almost looks vertical in places. Runners reach 500 feet (152 metres) above sea level at the highest point, take a deep downhill section into Tattenham Corner, the bend before a straight of nearly half a mile, and finish going upwards.

Tesio knew that Epsom remains the ultimate test of balance and resilience as well as class. There might be many lightly-raced colts which fail to handle the course but the cream has risen to the top and genes passed on through the ages, spanning from Diomed through The Flying Dutchman, Ormonde, Hyperion and Sea Bird to today's most influential sire, Galileo.

Epsom holds other races during the year, although the absence of a circuit restricts events to a mile and a half or shorter. The Great Metropolitan Handicap, once prestigious but now a semi-forgotten middle-tier contest at the

spring meeting, crossed over on the infield in order to stretch it to two and a quarter miles. The old place still gets by with a string of evening and Bank Holiday meetings with a separate Derby for amateurs and jump jockeys.

The real Derby, on the first weekend in June, is of course still its *raison d'etre*. The crowd is never recorded in the middle of the course and

ABOVE AND RIGHT: Two views giving perspectives on the uphill finish at the 2016 Investec Derby as Pat Smullen wins on Harzand.

is probably of nowhere near the proportions it might have been a century ago, but the roads and railways are brought to a standstill as many thousands gather amid the funfair, open-top buses and old-fashioned stalls.

Facilities have been given a much-needed upgrade. The paddock, which was once a brisk walk past the winning post, was moved closer when the white-storied Queen's Stand was opened in 1992 and the Duchess's Stand followed in 2009. A hotel now sits where the paddock once was.

Epsom is no longer one of the foremost training centres but there are still a dozen active stables dotted around, and racehorses can be spotted crossing the roads to use the gallops in the middle of the track. Staff members can sometimes be spotted in the Rubbing House, an attractive Victorian pub a little way past the winning post. It claims to be the only hostelry

in the world to be on a racecourse, with origins tracing back to earlier than the Derby itself. Since the middle of the eighteenth century, the name of the Derby winner has been chalked onto the wishing well of the Amato, a pub down the road in Epsom's town centre.

ABOVE: Open-top buses are one of the traditional visitors to Epsom, parking against the inside rails.

LEFT: Entrance to the Queen's Stand (left) on Derby Day requires gentlemen to be dressed in morning suit. Thankfully such rules do not apply through the rest of the season.

Exeter

Devon, England

Britain's racecourses are the most varied of any in the world, from the grassroots rural tracks up to the flagship arenas. Exeter sits in the former category and has two distinctions. Perched on the wooded Haldon Hill above the cathedral city, its altitude of 850 feet (259 metres) above sea level makes it the highest in the country. And the undulating oval of two miles is the longest jumps circuit in Britain, only shorter than Pontefract's Flat course in the overall category.

Horses know they have had a race after running at Exeter, which usually offers stamina-sapping ground during its meetings in the winter months. They disappear from sight on the back straight and then have a long uphill run to the finish.

The heath section on the infield has sometimes been used as a caravan park, disrupting the view further, but the frequent arrival of thick fog makes things considerably worse.

The racecourse is another legacy of horse-mad Charles II, who introduced the sport in the seventeenth century, while the first precise use of the present site is believed to be in 1769. Flat racing was originally held here but with one exception, this is no longer the case. A special event for Clydesdale horses is organized annually when the professional jump jockeys gamely attempt to ride the gentle giants and raise funds for the Devon Air Ambulance.

Exeter is not only about the fresh air. Many of the leading jumps trainers are based in Somerset and Devon and they consider it a valuable racecourse to initiate young horses, so there is always the chance of seeing a future star. There are 11 fences, a mixture of ditches and ordinary fences as well as a water jump.

Best Mate won his first steeplechase here in 2000 before clinching three consecutive Cheltenham Gold Cups. Henrietta Knight's handsome gelding also landed the track's annual showpiece, the Haldon Gold Cup, only to perish from a suspected heart attack in the same race in 2005.

He has a race named in his honour while another National Hunt hero Denman, who also began his career over fences at Exeter in 2006, is acknowledged by a bar. So do trainer Martin Pipe, jockey Sir Tony McCoy and Desert Orchid, another junior graduate at Exeter who became an unprecedented nationwide crowd favourite. The elegant Travado, who managed a hat-trick in the Haldon Gold Cup in the mid-1990s, must make do with his name on a corporate box.

Winners are not always easy to find but they came easily to Steve Whiteley in March 2011. The heating engineer had gone to the races on the bus armed with a free promotional ticket and invested £2 in a jackpot pool bet. Somehow he picked all six correct horses at generous odds, mostly on hunches and names he recognized, and scooped a record-breaking dividend £1,450,000.

OPPOSITE: Kieran Edgar riding Tom Parker (right) wins the much-loved Exeter Racecourse Clydesdale Stakes in 2014.

RIGHT: A more conventional hurdles race from January 2017 with a familiar hint of mist.

Flemington

Melbourne, Australia

There have been race meetings held on the banks of the Maribyrnong River since before Melbourne even became a city. Scotsman James Watson acquired the land, first by squatting and later by a more formal purchase, and named the house he built Flemington after his wife's family home in Morayshire.

The racecourse, which held its first meeting in 1840, soon picked up the Flemington title and was moved under the auspices of the Victoria Racing Club. Its infrastructure quickly improved and a marsh in the middle of the track was drained. By 1854, a spring meeting joined the original autumn fixture. The seeds of the Melbourne Cup, which began in 1861 and quickly became an Australian institution, had been sewn. Six-figure crowds were very soon making their way to the flatlands a little way north of the city centre and congregating on the hill, and that has remained the case to this day.

Flemington has adapted to the desires of today's racegoer while remaining respectful of its past. The backdrop of skyscrapers is a reminder of Melbourne's position as a vibrant, modern city, but Victorians are still quite an old-fashioned, conservative bunch as a rule. The winners of the Melbourne Cup still pass through large wrought iron gates on their return from the track. Bluestone walls from the 1880s have been retained, and the remnants of the old grandstand form the foundations of the present Hill structure.

Some change has been necessary. The Members' Old Grandstand, which had palpably reached the end of the road after 92 years' service, will be replaced by a curving tiered Club stand more in line with the other facilities on offer. But while some will choose to dine sky-high with panoramic views from the Atrium, others will always stick with the wood-panelled splendour of the Members' Dining Room or, better still, among the oil paintings of the ultra-exclusive Committee Room.

The 127-hectare (313 acres) site has been engulfed by suburban Melbourne and many of the leading Australian trainers, including the charismatic former actress Gai Waterhouse, use the village of stables on the south-eastern part of the course. In the middle are a selection of training gallops. The track itself is pear-shaped and around a mile and a half in circumference with wide and sweeping bends.

RIGHT: An aerial view of the racecourse shows its proximity to downtown Melbourne and its adjacency to the Maribyrnong River.

BELOW: The unmistakeable finishing post at Flemington.

BOTTOM: The start of the 2016 Emirates Melbourne Cup won by Almandin and ridden by Kerrin McEvoy.

Nationwide racing interest is condensed into the four days of the Spring Carnival at Flemington around the first week of November. Some 16,000 roses lining the walkways and paddocks must be pampered to bloom in time with the occasion and a plethora of marquees are erected.

The Cup is held on a Tuesday, and it has become a state holiday. Many will have already been to Victoria Derby Day on the Saturday. The card is full of Group 1 races and has a traditional black and white theme for ladies' dresses, while men can take a chance with the changeable local climate and wear morning suits. The full spectrum of celebrities have attended the festival over the years, from British model Jean Shrimpton, who caused quite a stir when arriving in a short white shift dress 1965, to record-breaking sprinter Usain Bolt. Racing dominates the front and back pages of the newspapers and there is even a parade of the jockeys and trainers through the main shopping streets to Federation Square.

Folk heroes like 12-times winning trainer and 'Cups King' Bart Cummings and the giant chestnut of the 1930s Phar Lap, who remains Australia's greatest horse, have statues at Flemington.

When Vintage Crop, for Irishman Dermot Weld, became the first overseas-trained winner in 1993, it opened up a truly international competition. It might be technically a two-mile handicap but the prize money of nearly £4 million attracts top-class stayers from Europe and Asia.

RIGHT: The running of the Melbourne Cup is a truly nation-stopping event. Employers reckon its costs AUS $1.2 billion in lost productvity.

BELOW: The Visit Victoria Plate is one of the support races on Melbourne Cup Day.

Soma-Nomaoi Samurai Festival

Fukushima, Japan

The roots of British racing and even the Palio di Siena are made to look almost modern compared with the events re-enacted at this three-day celebration of the samurai at the Hibarigahara Festival Site in Minamisoma, a city on the north-eastern coast of Honshu.

The slogan of the Soma-Nomaoi is that it is 'weaving a tradition of over 1000 years', beginning with the time of the clan leader Masakado in the tenth century, who released wild horses on the plains and ordered his cavalry to catch and offer them to the gods as part of a military exercise.

Held on the final Saturday, Sunday and Monday in July, it is considered a passing-on of Japan's history to younger generations, with ceremonies and parades in authentic dress and many Shinto rituals which are beyond simple explanation.

Sunday's Kacchu Keiba is one of the two crowd-pleasing highlights of the three days. The sounding of a conch shell and the beating of drums at noon signal the start of the event for the samurai warriors in full uniform to take part in horse races. There are 10 heats of 10 runners, with riders carrying katana swords and ancestral banners, around a sand loop of five furlongs.

Over 40,000 people sit on the grass, in what is normally very hot weather, to enjoy the races, which are followed by the Shinki Soudatsusen, the crescendo of an ancient battle re-creation.

The same riders gather together in the middle of the field and fireworks explode, dropping flags down from the sky which they compete to grab. The 40 winners ride up a winding slope and present their flags as an offering to a local shrine.

Minamisoma, an area rich in horse-breeding tradition, has suffered wretchedly of late. It sustained horrific damage from the earthquake-generated tsunami in 2011, not only to buildings and infrastructure, but because of the triggering of the disaster at the Fukushima Daiichi nuclear power station just 15 miles down the road. Many hundreds died, and others whose properties were within the exclusion zone remain evacuated. The festival, which is close to affected areas, remains a vital part of its identity and has continued to run.

LEFT: Horsemen look to the sky as they compete for the sacred flag (Shinki Soudatsusen).

OPPOSITE: Samurai horsemen compete in the Kacchu Keiba, or armed horse race.

LEFT: Holding their katana swords Samurai horsemen pray during a ceremony at the Soma Nomaoi Festival. Apart from the horse racing and flag competition, ancient battle scenes are re-created from the Sengoku Period (1477-1573).

ABOVE AND OPPOSITE: In a centuries-old tradition, horsemen compete in the Kacchu Keiba in full body armour.

Galway

Ballybrit, Galway, Ireland

Ballybrit racecourse, as it is better known locally, hosts Ireland's longest, most vaunted and bacchanalian racing festival. Galway is officially a city with a population of 80,000 but around 250,000 will attend during the week. Few have the stamina to make it through every afternoon and night from the last Monday in July to the first Sunday in August.

There seems to have always been an attraction about the place; it is said that 40,000 people turned up for the very first meeting in 1869. There had previously been racing elsewhere in the region and the land for the racecourse was donated from the wealthy estate of Captain Wilson Lynch. Given most credit for its founding, though, is Lord St Lawrence, the local MP and chairman of the stewards. The Midland and Great Western Railway offered to bring horses to the meeting for free, which guaranteed large fields.

The meeting hosted the first running of the Galway Plate, which remains one of Ireland's most famous races to this day. No longer jumping walls, as in the inaugural version, the Plate headlines the meeting on the Wednesday and is a fiercely competitive two-and-three-quarter-mile handicap chase.

The Summer Festival meeting is a mixture of chases, hurdles and Flat events, many of which are low-key. The Galway Hurdle, somewhat appropriately sponsored by Guinness, is the feature of Thursday's crowded ladies' day and was Ireland's most valuable jump race for many years. What the races have in common is that they are mostly won by Dermot Weld, the meeting's nearly constant top trainer since the early 1980s. There are usually 49 races and in 2011, he took 17 of them.

Weld's Ansar was a standing dish at the course, winning one Galway Hurdle and two Plates. He was retired in 2008 after finishing third in the latter, one victory short of the all-time record of three set by Tipperary Boy at the turn of the previous century.

The course is shaped in a rough rectangle, a mile and a quarter long. There are no chase fences in the short home straight but the penultimate and final obstacles, running sharply downhill, are believed to be the closest together of any in the world. A horse would only take five strides between them.

As the showcase meeting retains its popularity, Galway has moved with the times. The Corrib stand, built in 1955, had a pub underneath it which claimed to have the longest bar in the world. It was replaced by the more spacious Millennium Stand in 1999.

Then, fitted in between the 2006 and 2007 Festivals, an even more impressive structure arrived. The Killanin Stand (main photo), designed by EPR Architects, cost €22 million and has a capacity of 6,000. The lozenge-shaped building has an innovative look to it, with a cantilevered steel roof, and curved windows in the corner. Care was taken to ensure that a good proportion is open for ordinary racegoers, with corporate hospitality at the top. It is named after the revered Lord Killanin, a former International Olympic Committee president and powerhouse chairman of Galway, and also the father of renowned trainer Mouse Morris.

TOP: Ballybrit Castle can be found in the centre of the course.

RIGHT AND OPPOSITE: The beautiful curve of the Killanin Stand designed by EPR Architects.

Garrison Savannah

Bridgetown, Barbados

The naming of the only racecourse in Barbados is self-explanatory but becomes even more apparent when visiting. It is steeped in military history and the course is now part of a historic conservation area on the outskirts of the capital, Bridgetown.

There has been some form of defence headquarters on the site since the island became a British colony in the seventeenth century. A garrison was created with the arrival of permanently stationed troops in 1780. The racecourse area served as the parade ground and there are early reports of races being held between the officers and their horses from around 1845.

Interest grew, and wealthy traders, merchants and plantation owners were invited to join in the sport. The withdrawal of forces in 1905 saw the attractive surrounding buildings, many of imported brick, pass into local hands and the Barbados Turf Club was founded to run the track.

Standing out proudly on one corner of the home straight is the red chiming clock tower of the Main Guard (main photo) and in front of it are 26 cannon. Since the early twentieth century, Garrison Savannah has housed a large cannon collection, some dating back to 1620, with examples from Sweden and Holland.

The rarest, the Commonwealth cannon, is one of only two bearing Oliver Cromwell's crest, the other being in the Tower of London. Two sentries, dressed in a white, red and black colonial uniform, stand outside the Main Guard and there is a colourful changing of the guard ceremony at noon, involving retired members of the Barbados Defence Force.

Racing at The Garrison is typically full of Caribbean hospitality and informality. The track remains a fine piece of greensward with a sand gallop inside. It is pear-shaped and extremely tight at a circumference of only six furlongs.

It has three small stands with some grand members' facilities, with others preferring to picnic under the trees or enjoy some of the local delicacies such as pudding and souse, a curious mixture of pork, pickles and sweet potato.

There is usually a break during September and October but there are meetings on most alternate Saturdays through the rest of the year. The most important race is the Barbados Gold Cup, run over nine furlongs at the end of February or start of March. It is sponsored by Sandy Lane, the luxurious nearby resort which has long been associated with the Coolmore set of John Magnier, Michael Tabor and Derrick Smith. Many other wealthy businesspeople who spend part of their year on the island have horses including British fund manager Sir Martyn Arbib and his wife Lady Sally, whose Blast of Storm won the Gold Cup three times.

Sir David Seale, producer of one of the island's leading rum brands, is president of the racecourse and one of its leading owners. Garrison Savannah has a few exports of its own to boast of, too. Sir Michael Stoute, multiple British champion Flat trainer, found his way into racing, quite literally, as his father was deputy commissioner of police and the racecourse could be accessed by climbing over a ladder and over the garden wall of the family home. Stoute's success on the track brought a knighthood for services to Barbadian tourism and sport.

ABOVE: A large field for the Sandy Lane Gold Cup.

Hipodromo da Gavea

Rio de Janeiro, Brazil

No racecourse in the world can have appeared in as many postcard pictures, even if it tends not to be the main subject. Gavea sits among all of Rio de Janeiro's most recognizable landmarks and, most strikingly of all, beneath the Corcovado mountain upon which the outstretched Christ the Redeemer stands. It was seen frequently in panning shots for the 2016 Olympics from its position in an upmarket district near the banks of the Rodrigo de Freitas Lagoon.

It is not just a distant piece of eye-candy; Gavea is a well-preserved reminder of the Roaring Twenties. The city's racecourse was once in an area further north which is now the world-famous Maracana football stadium but a replacement, modelled on Longchamp in Paris, was opened after six years of construction in 1926.

The entrance, from the original design by French architect André Raimbert, could easily belong to an art gallery or fine museum. Inside, it still seems extraordinary that the patterned marble floors and decadent staircases should belong to a racecourse. The elegant, wood-panelled bars and the benches looking onto the track make it feel like a private members' club.

The grandstands were built to hold 70,000 people but, as so sadly seems the case with many of these great theatres, Gavea had its heyday some time ago when the carioca would flock to see the maestro Luiz Rigoni riding in the 1950s and 60s. It can still get 30,000 for June's Grande Premio Brasil, the signature race which offers a guaranteed spot at the Breeders' Cup, but there are fixtures scheduled four days a week for the entire year and they usually only attract the die-hards.

Gavea is flat and, from above, its two dirt tracks look like a paperclip. They are surrounded by a turf circuit of around a mile and three furlongs. On the back stretch is stabling for around 1500 horses.

Footballers will probably always dominate Brazil's list of sporting exports but it is a country that continues to generate fine horsemen. João Moreira, the 'Magic Man' of Asian racing, and British champion Silvestre de Sousa both transferred from the Sao Paulo circuit to fly the green, yellow and blue flag across the world.

The most prolific of Brazilian riders hails from Rio. Jorge Ricardo, a graduate of Gavea's renowned jockey school, collected 25 consecutive Brazilian titles beginning in 1982 and managed as many as 477 victories in one season. He was for many years engaged in a battle with American Russell Baze as to who was the winning-most rider of all-time. In an indication of the weakening financial clout of Brazilian racing, Ricardo relocated to break further records in Buenos Aires.

Brazil's breeding industry is widely respected and its durable horses are popular in America. Leroidesanimaux spent his formative years at Gavea, later winning a prestigious Eclipse Award as 2005's best U.S. turf performer. Gloria de Campeao also began at the track and won the 2010 Dubai World Cup in the care of Frenchman Pascal Bary.

Goodwood

West Sussex, England

Goodwood would be many aficionados' choice as the most beautiful setting for a racecourse in the world. The grandstand offers an unrivalled view of the Sussex Downs without a building in sight, and looking in the opposite direction, south of the paddock, even the Isle Of Wight can be picked out in the distance. It sits in the verdant 12,000-acre (4,850 hectares) estate of the Duke of Richmond, which includes Goodwood House with its mixture of classical, Palladian and Regency-style features, a private airfield and famed motor-racing circuit, golf course and parkland.

The racecourse was created in 1802 by the third Duke, an Army field marshal, to keep his troops happy and occupied rather than of any close personal interest. The public later began to enjoy the annual event and the main meeting of the year, for five days between late July and early August, has been coined 'Glorious Goodwood' for as long as anyone can remember. King Edward VII, who described Glorious Goodwood as "a garden party with racing tacked on" set the

trend of wearing a linen suit and Panama hat in 1906 and his style has prevailed ever since.

The estate is currently run by the innovative 11th Duke (formerly the Earl of March), and operates in a more commercial manner with events such as the Festival of Speed and the Revival on the motor circuit. It even sells Panamas in its own red and yellow livery, and the genteel nature of the racecourse has not been lost.

RIGHT: A general view of the finishing post and the glorious Sussex countryside at the Qatar Goodwood Festival of 2015.

BELOW: Ryan Moore on Master of the World eases down after winning the Betfred Mile Handicap Stakes at the 2017 Goodwood Festival.

Glorious Goodwood remains traditional if not overtly elitist. A smart dress code must be followed in the Richmond Enclosure but other stands are more relaxed. It is free to sit on the slopes of Trundle Hill and watch the action head-on.

There are many more meetings at Goodwood than in the past, but practice does not make perfect for even the best of riders on a track that will always challenge. It follows the contours of the land with a sweeping downhill right-handed bend into a four-furlong run towards the winning post. For the occasional marathon race over two and a half miles, runners gather in front of the stands and run in the opposite direction up the home straight, turn around in the distance and eventually come back again.

Goodwood's most prestigious race, the Group 1 Sussex Stakes, was so uncompetitive when inaugurated as a two-year-old sprint that it would regularly be a walkover with one runner. It has latterly become the point where the best three-year-old milers from the Guineas meet the older generation and has been won by such superstars as Brigadier Gerard and Frankel.

Although there are other top-class races through the week, such as the venerable Goodwood and Stewards' Cups, another appeal of the

festival it that it also has some less important makeweight contests in between and never feels as frenetically-paced as Royal Ascot.

To emphasize this leisurely spirit, even the journey is worthwhile. The Chichester train makes slow progress from London but chugs through wonderful sections of countryside near the River Arun. Those in a car can take a scenic option for the final stages which pass by Goodwood House and the motor-racing circuit on the way up.

Unfortunately, it lives and dies by the weather. In the cold and wet, Goodwood is miserably exposed and the occasional sea fret drifting across from the English Channel can cause havoc and even abandonment. But on a sunny afternoon, a spectator can feel like the luckiest person on earth as they look out over the Downs and contemplate stopping off at one of the picture-perfect pubs nearby, like The Royal Oak at East Lavant or The Fox Goes Free just a tootle down the hill at Charlton.

BELOW LEFT: Along with Henley and Wimbledon, Goodwood is the perfect summer venue for strawberries and cream.

BELOW: A side view of the Sussex Stand, part of the Gordon Enclosure, a slightly less formal enclosure than the Richmond.

BOTTOM: Frankie Dettori (in yellow and green) on Lancelot du Lac races home in front of the field and thunder clouds in the Stewards' Cup at the 2017 Festival.

RIGHT: The combination of an undulating track and large fields can make Goodwood a difficult place to find a winner.

Happy Valley

Hong Kong

Present-day Happy Valley must offer a vastly different panorama to the original one, which was opened in 1846 in the days when Hong Kong was a British colony. The trees which led gently up to the peaks of Hong Kong Island have given way to skyscrapers and apartment blocks, jostling for position in one of the most densely populated areas on earth.

The British rulers of the time decided that this previously uninhabitable tract of swampland known locally as Wong Nai Chung would be the perfect place for a racecourse and it was drained to provide sport, with a wooden grandstand and other temporary facilities.

Tragedy struck during the annual meeting in 1918 when bamboo-mat sheds collapsed, upsetting cooking ranges and causing a fire which resulted in the loss of nearly 600 lives.

Club rules were revised in 1926 to allow Chinese membership and racing continued to grow in popularity. Until the fairly recent creation of the territory's second racecourse at Sha Tin, a vast international venue in the New Territories, horses were also trained at Happy Valley and it was a common sight to see them being led in and out of multi-storey stable blocks overlooking the track.

Meetings on a Wednesday night under the floodlights are a wonderfully atmospheric experience. A seven-storey stand lines the short home straight of an oval grass course which is less than a mile in circumference and even a run-of-the-mill card can attract a crowd of 20,000, with ex-pats and tourists lured in by cheap entrance fees and beer.

The reason many of the locals go is to gamble and the turnover on the Hong Kong Jockey

LEFT: Jockey Karis Teetan celebrates his win on High Velocity in the 2017 Jardine Handicap at Happy Valley.

Club's state monopolized tote system is truly eye-watering with nearly £100m staked on individual meetings. On non-racing days, it is just as busy on the infield with pitches laid out for rugby, football and hockey.

Most of the top names in Flat racing, such as Lester Piggott and Ryan Moore, have taken lucrative retainers to ride in Hong Kong during the winter months but the tight nature of the Happy Valley course makes it a difficult one for any rider to master. Some of the best are offered the chance to prove themselves at the International Jockey Championship each December prior to Sha Tin's huge annual showpiece event.

ABOVE AND TOP: Night racing in a busy city is a tremendously atmospheric experience.

LEFT: Many racecourses sit on land valuable to developers, but on the densely populated Hong Kong island the real estate value would be incalculable.

Hoppegarten

Brandenburg, Berlin, Germany

It seems somewhat ironic that Hoppegarten, virtually hidden from view for many years on the eastern side of the Berlin Wall, owes its rebirth to private enterprise.

The grande-dame of German racing was established by the Prussian aristocrats of the Union-Klub (the equivalent of the British Jockey Club), replacing the hop fields which provide its name, and was opened in 1868 by King Wilhelm I and Chancellor Otto von Bismarck. It quickly became the home of all the Classics bar the Derby, plus another sequence of important Group races attracting top runners from abroad. The neighbouring training centre was soon filled with 1,200 horses.

Racing continued through both World Wars but a stunning blow was delivered by the division of Germany in 1945. When Hoppegarten came under Soviet control, most of the best horses were moved west and the Union-Klub, considered to be an enemy of the working class, was exiled to Cologne.

Yet still they raced on at Hoppegarten, as there were enough people in the German Democratic Republic who were interested in the sport. The racecourse was maintained and the operation was entirely state financed, with around 20 small-scale trainers.

After the Wall came down, it hosted a reunification meeting in 1990 which drew 40,000 from both sides of the former iron curtain. Sponsors flooded in and everything looked rosy for a few months until the realization that the local economy would not recover as quickly as expected. Confusion over who actually owned Hoppegarten rumbled on and it was down to just a small handful of meetings by 2008.

A saviour arrived in the shape of Gerhard Schoningh, a racing enthusiast who had just made his fortune selling his London fund management business. After intensive negotiation, Schoningh bought the site and Hoppegarten became Germany's only privately-owned racecourse.

He had bought one of the most beautifully-preserved tracks in Europe, with so much potential, being just a 25-minute journey from central Berlin. Hoppegarten is entirely surrounded by woodland and its Bauhaus-style grandstand buildings from the 1920s are listed. It is a place where time stands still on the crisp gravel paths and under the giant trees in the paddock and public spaces.

The track itself is lined by hedges and is in a soft diamond shape of just under a mile and a half. It is a fair and galloping course with a gentle uphill finish. There is no jumping at present but a number of old fences remain standing, a little sombrely, in the middle.

To his great credit, the urbane Schoningh has not tried to reinvent the wheel and recognizes that the greenery and historic buildings are Hoppegarten's greatest selling point. It was in dire need of refurbishment but modernization has been gentle, more through a touch of the paintbrush, a few flowers and improved utilities.

Almost all the course's key races had migrated to other parts of Germany and a clear sign of the track's recovery was when the Grosser Preis von Berlin returned home in 2011. This Group 1 event over a mile and a half has been showcasing the best of the stamina-rich domestic breed since 1888 but was moved to Dusseldorf in 1947 and lost its old name for 30 years.

Significant investment has been made in the training facilities, which are considered the finest in Germany, and worthy of comparison with Newmarket or Chantilly. There are walking and exercise tracks within Hoppegarten's extensive woodland and the company purchased another even bigger site at nearby Neuenhagen with the intention that once again it will become the country's leading training centre.

RIGHT: Jump racing has declined in Germany but it is hoped that it will return as part of the gradual upgrading of facilities.

BELOW: Hoppegarten's showcase race, the Group 1 Grosser Preis von Berlin is back at its rightful home.

Keeneland

Kentucky, America

Besides being one of America's premier racecourses, Keeneland is also home to the country's most important horse sales company.

Set in what has grown to more than 1000 acres (405 hectares) of landscaped Bluegrass countryside, it is a sporting institution and, indeed, appears on the Register of National Historic Places. The land had belonged to the Keene family from 1783 and Jack Keene was using some of it to develop his own private racing and training facility from the 1920s when the site came to the attention of a group of prominent breeders headed by Hal Price Headley and Major Louis Beard.

Lexington in central Kentucky, America's horse racing capital, was without a racecourse after the closure of the city's dilapidated central racecourse in 1933. As Keene had already begun work on the infrastructure but had run out of resources, they came to an arrangement with him for the land. After only 15 months of around-the-

clock work, Keeneland was open for business in October 1936 and 8,000 travelled to the site just west of the city to see the first meeting.

In Headley and Beard's initial prospectus, they outlined their desire to "create a model race track to perpetuate and improve the sport and to provide a course that is intended to serve as a symbol of the fine traditions of thoroughbred racing."

The two men would approve of what stands today, as their project has become a place that is not only stunningly beautiful but protective of its heritage. There is a dedicated bugler to announce races and the committee did not even permit broadcasting of commentaries over a public address system until 1997 as it might ruin the tranquil atmosphere.

BELOW: Miniature jockeys are individually painted in the colours of each of Keeneland's Grade One winners every year.

One of the most notable aspects has been the planting of the trees, which are at their best for the track's two meetings for around three weeks in April and October. In spring, the dogwood, magnolia and redbud will be in bloom, while oak and maple add their vibrant autumnal hues. The paddock, lined by hedges, surrounds a splendid old sycamore tree.

Both meetings are full of top-class races around a dirt oval of just longer than a mile, with a tighter turf course inside that stages a few jumps races. A record of 50,000, many viewing from temporary facilities, attended when Keeneland was selected to host the 2015 Breeders' Cup.

Many horses that race there were sold at Keeneland sales, which gained momentum from 1943 when there was a wartime restriction on travel and instead of Kentucky breeders sending their young horses to go under the hammer in Saratoga, they did it in a tent in the Keeneland paddock. The sales company has become a proverbial money tree, responsible for producing countless winners of the likes of the Kentucky Derby.

There are four major dates and the September Yearling Sale is the centrepiece, attracting buyers from around the world. In 2006 Sheikh Mohammed of Dubai paid $11.7 million for a colt he named Meydan City. Such investment is no guarantee of success; Meydan City won two small races in England and recouped only £24,104 in prize money!

As well as its sales complex and the associated stabling facilities and training track, Keeneland has a shop selling its own merchandise and even a library which has become one of the main resource centres for researching the thoroughbred with 300,000 books, journals and catalogues as well as a vast archive of newspaper cuttings, photographs and films.

ABOVE: The beautifully landscaped gardens are open to the public every day, regardless of whether there is a race event or not. There are a number of different tours that can be taken, including a 'Behind-the-Scenes Sales Tour' and a 'Behind-the-Scenes Racing Tour'.

OPPOSITE: Keeneland was added to the National Register of Historic Places in 1986. A large number of scenes from the 2003 movie *Seabiscuit* were shot here.

Kenilworth

Cape Town, South Africa

South Africa's oldest racecourse, opened in 1882, has many assets which make it stand out from the crowd. Sitting in the heart of Cape Town, it has the benefit of the city's astounding topography. Behind the grandstand is the majestic Table Mountain and out in the distance in the other direction are views of the Hawequas and the Hottentots Holland ranges.

Kenilworth itself has its own natural attraction in the infield of the pear-shaped racecourse. It looks like an ordinary piece of heathland, but is, in fact, one of the few remaining examples of Cape Flats Sand Fynbos, a lowland vegetation unique to the area and most of which has been destroyed by development.

The Fynbos is home to critically endangered ericaceous plants, a breed of peregrine falcon and a number of rare amphibians including the Cape Flats frog, or micro frog, which is the size of a thumbnail. So the racecourse is now the dedicated Kenilworth Racecourse Conservation Area and is entirely protected.

It is also the hub of perhaps the best racing in the country and the track, which holds races up to a mile and a quarter and is bisected by a six-furlong straight sprint, has immaculately kept grass for its main season between October and February.

Late January's Sun Met meeting has become the most valuable race day on the continent, featuring four Group 1 races. A couple of weeks earlier the feature race is the Queen's Plate, which was inaugurated by the South African Turf Club in 1861, with the winner receiving a silver platter and 50 guineas.

The Plate was held at Green Point Common until the opening of Kenilworth in what is now an affluent southern suburb, and it is not only South Africa's oldest race but the longest-running sporting event in the country.

Racing does have a somewhat louche reputation among the general public even if the sport is underpinned by the support of a few refined breeders and owners, mostly of European descent and recession-proof wealth. Kenilworth's midweek meeting will take place in front of a handful of spectators but efforts have been made to make some of the main weekend events more socially aspirational.

It is certainly a pleasant place to while away an afternoon if Cape Town's weather gods are in a benevolent mood. The paddock area, watched over by an old pavilion, is shaded by various interesting trees and there is plenty of space to shelter from the sun or rain. The grandstand and clubhouse have become a little dated but the influential owners plan to provide a much-needed upgrade.

There is a robust breeding industry with many of the major stud farms within a couple of hours' drive of Cape Town. Quarantine restrictions have not always made it easy for horses to travel abroad if they have outgrown domestic competition, but there has been plenty of success in Asia and the Gulf. Variety Club cut his teeth at Kenilworth before winning valuable Group races in Dubai and Hong Kong in 2014.

The country has perhaps been more famous for producing riders. Michael Roberts and Basil Marcus were both born in the Cape and became champion jockeys at home before repeating that feat in Britain and Hong Kong respectively.

FAR LEFT: Bernard Fayd'Herbe and Futura claim the 2015 renewal of the J&B (now Sun) Met, one of South Africa's biggest races.

LEFT: Runners and riders gather in the charming tree-covered Kenilworth paddock.

ABOVE RIGHT: Hospitality tents are assembled at the start of Met day in 2017.

RIGHT: Kenilworth crowds are sparse for a midweek meeting but racegoers will turn out on an important Saturday.

Kiplingcotes

Yorkshire, England

Britain's oldest horse race does not take place at one of the country's great sporting institutions, like Cheltenham, Ascot or Chester. Instead it takes place on a racecourse in the ancient countryside of the Yorkshire Wolds, near the small town of Market Weighton.

The Kiplingcotes Derby has, by common consent, been held there since 1519, although the first sworn testimony that it took place is from 1555. Records, and a strict set of rules, were drawn up a century later.

It always takes place on the third Thursday in March and is open to anyone who turns up at the winning post, at what looks like a footpath signpost at Londesborough Wold Farm by 11am. Entrants simply require the £4.25 fee and their horse must be carrying a minimum of 10st.

They then walk or trot up to the starting post near the disused Kiplingcotes train station, and once a handkerchief is waved by the starter at noon, runners head off in nearly a straight line for four miles.

Many moons ago there was a proper racecourse at Kiplingcotes but nowadays the Derby field gallop uphill and down, along tracks, verges and muddy sections of fields and at one point even cross a main road.

It is a tradition of which the folk of the East Riding are proud, and hundreds will come out to watch at various sections of the course, even if it is impossible to see the whole race. Expenses have increased for stewarding and policing in the modern health and safety-conscious era but the race is considered an important local tourist attraction. On occasion, a brave bookmaker will attend to take bets.

About 10 minutes later, the first of what tends to be about a dozen keen local amateurs will pass the winning post. They will be rewarded with £50 and a trophy but the peculiarities continue as the runner-up receives all of the entrance fees, which can be even more than the winner's prize in a well-attended year.

There has never been a break in the Derby being held, and for good reason. It is stated in its constitution that if the race does not take place one year, it never will again. The weather is not always clement but there was such horrendous snow and ice in 1947 that one farmer had to complete the course alone. Even during the outbreak of foot and mouth disease, when livestock was not to be moved, another of the local enthusiasts walked their horse through to ensure the legacy of the race continued.

TOP AND OPPOSITE: The Derby is run over a variety of roads, farm tracks and fields, a course that stretches four miles.

ABOVE: The signpost boasts the age of the race.

Kranji

Singapore

The Singapore Turf Club cannot be accused of not moving with the times, certainly in a literal sense. When the twenty-first century arrived it abandoned Bukit Timah, a rambling old place that could fit 50,000 and had been home to the city state's racing since 1933. It ushered in Kranji, built in the greener north of the island near the straits border with Malaysia.

Kranji is the quintessential modern racecourse. It is landscaped, spacious, cheap for the general public but also offering luxury if one wants to pay, and it is effortlessly easy to access via Singapore's Mass Rapid Transit train system. It is particularly proud of its main grandstand with a roof which, viewed from the air, is supposed to resemble a horse galloping. There are five tiers and a capacity of 30,000. Air conditioning is essential everywhere in this humid country and even the horses benefit from it in the 1,600-box stabling facility.

Meetings are held most Friday evenings under the lights and on Sunday afternoons. The 25 registered trainers at Kranji's permanent stabling facilities can exercise their horses either on the racecourse or on five dedicated gallops tracks. The turf course is wide at 100 feet (31 metres), a mile and a quarter in circumference. There is also a shorter loop, with an artificial Polytrack surface inside. They are bordered by tropical rainforest.

Gambling, which used to be allowed only at the races, is a big deal in Singapore. Annual turnover is over $1.5 billion and punters mass on the ground floor areas, watching not only the local racing but televised action from the rest of Asia and even further afield. Casinos were allowed to open in 2010 but the perverse nature of Singaporean laws mean neither they, nor the racecourse, are permitted to advertise their wares.

For 15 years after its opening, Kranji held a race meeting open to overseas competition every May. The $3 million Singapore International Airlines Cup was taken by such decent animals as British-trained Grandera and Hong Kong's Military Attack but was discontinued after the organizers decided it had been successful enough in raising the sport's profile and quality.

Many of the leading competitors are recruited from overseas. British jockey Alan Munro has been an ever-present for many years and was joined by a number of Australians.

New Zealander Laurie Laxon has been a regular champion trainer and has won every race of significance, but perhaps the scene's finest recent ambassador has actually been a horse. Rocket Man was unbeaten in 17 starts at home and flew the flag abroad by becoming the nation's first ever overseas Group 1 winner in Dubai. The hardy old sprinter was finally retired, aged 11, in 2016 to take up residence in South Africa.

BELOW LEFT: November's Singapore Gold Cup is now considered the most prestigious race while the 2006 Queen Elizabeth II Cup was watched by Her Majesty in person.

BELOW: The parade ring is just one example of the perfectly executed facilities at Kranji.

RIGHT: Night training and night meetings are an essential part of racing in the steaming Singapore climate.

accident involving injury to several jockeys and several horses in 1994 prompted a safety review. Presently, the events are sprint handicaps over six and seven furlongs and the horses and riders must be experienced. Many of the best-known domestic figures have been involved, including jockey Ruby Walsh and trainer Dermot Weld.

Simply getting the meeting on takes plenty of planning. It is not allowed to be in a school holiday and must happen six and a half hours after high tide. Kevin Coleman, the manager, and his voluntary committee are out monitoring the movements of sand on the beach in the days running in, and block storm water outlets and shovel sand into the right places over the final hours. Once racing is over, everything must be hastily dismantled before the water returns.

Despite seeming in such a precarious spot, Laytown is rarely abandoned and around 5,000 people make their way down for a very different day at the beach.

TOP: A decision on the exact location of the course is only made at the last minute when the committee can judge the positioning of the shifting sandbanks.

ABOVE: Temporary rails are erected for the final run-in.

LEFT: Beach racing was quite common in Ireland at one time with races at Milltown Malbay in County Clare, Baltray and Termonfeckin. There is still racing on the beach at Omey Island, but not under Turf Club rules.

Leopardstown

Dublin, Ireland

A visit to Dublin's last remaining city racecourse evokes a real sense of nostalgia. It is accessed from the centre by travelling past the Georgian houses of the capital's smart southern suburbs, such as Ballsbridge and Rathgar, and on the journey one can easily imagine the scene on Leopardstown's opening day in 1888. Captain George Quin had purchased 200 acres (80 hectares) of cheap land and decided to build a track, supposedly based upon Sandown Park in England, albeit that Leopardstown races anticlockwise and the Esher venue is clockwise. Word had clearly spread as there was chaos on the roads and on the now defunct train line from Harcourt Street to the racecourse station at Foxrock, and reports of chaotic pushing and shoving to get through the gates.

By the early 1900s Leopardstown – the name derives from a leper hospital that was once in this area near the foot of the Dublin Mountains – had been taken over by Harold and Fred Clarke. Playwright Samuel Beckett was born within a stone's throw of the racecourse and his father, who was friendly with Fred Clarke, enjoyed an afternoon there. Beckett recalled walking around Leopardstown in his youth and made a number of references to it in his work.

His friend, and another giant of Irish literature, James Joyce mentions the racecourse in both *Finnegans Wake* and *Ulysses*, when Leopold Bloom tells Mrs Breen that, "Molly won seven shillings on a three-year-old named Nevertell and coming home along by Foxrock in that old fiveseater shanderadan of a waggonette

you were in your heyday then and you had on that new hat of white velours with a surround of molefur that Mrs Hayes advised you to buy because it was marked down to nineteen and eleven."

Leopardstown has long been Ireland's top mixed facility, offering top-class Flat and jumps racing. However, the popularity of the area for housing placed it in danger of falling into the hands of developers. In 1969, the Clarke family decided to sell it to what is now the governing body, Horse Racing Ireland, for only £300,000 – essentially just the land's agricultural value.

Parcels of it have been sold off over time and a straight sprint track was lost in 2001 with the construction of the M50 motorway but the fine, galloping oval of a mile and three-quarters remains a noted test for a horse. A fresh wind can blow in from the sea and the rather grey buildings are often matched by skies of the same colour, but it remains an atmospheric if unpretentious place.

Annual members get their money's worth through the year. The Flat season has early trial races for the Classics as well as Ireland's most important race, the Champion Stakes, which moved to Leopardstown after the closure of Dublin's Phoenix Park.

Held in early September, it draws the elite mile-and-a-quarter horses and has produced some memorable battles, chief of which was that between Fantastic Light and Galileo in 2001, and

a home-coming for Ireland's 2009 champion Sea The Stars.

The jumping at Leopardstown is rated more highly by the public, with the four-day Christmas Festival headed by the Lexus Chase, scene of the clashes between English and Irish heroes Best Mate and Beef Or Salmon in 2003 and 2004. The Irish Gold Cup and Champion Hurdle, held at the start of the year, were won on multiple occasions by such greats as Florida Pearl, Istabraq and Hurricane Fly.

BELOW: Jockey David Mullins has a bruising encounter with the Leopardstown turf as Identity Thief unseats him during the Frank Ward Solicitors Arkle Novice Steeplechase.

OPPOSITE: Fine weather for the 2016 Christmas Festival at Leopardstown as the field passes the grandstand for the first time in the Pertemps Network Handicap Hurdle.

Maisons-Laffitte

Paris, France

Placing a racecourse on the banks of one of Europe's largest rivers might not seem the most strategically sensible choice, but Maisons-Laffitte has lasted longer than any other venue in Paris.

The racecourse offers a very different test to others in France. The straight course, abutting the Seine and running right from left looking out from the grandstand, is equal with Newmarket in being as long as any other in Europe.

Spectators had better be paying attention as looking left from the winning post is another loop for longer races, making Maisons-Laffitte one of the few tracks to have action coming from both directions.

The racecourse was launched by Joseph Oller, the entrepreneur who invented modern parimutuel betting, and the organization later fell under the auspices of the French racing authorities. There has long been a horse culture in this part of the north-western Parisian suburbs, with hunting and later informal race meetings in the eighteenth century.

Maisons-Laffitte is twinned with Newmarket in England and is known as Cité du Cheval (City of the Horse). It was the biggest racehorse training centre – home to more than 1500 – before World War II. That number has halved due to loss of land and the growth of nearby Chantilly but it remains important, particularly to jumps trainers, with a number of training tracks in the parkland. It is a curious sight to see roadsigns allowing priority to horses so close to a capital city centre.

Jump racing has been discontinued, although there have often been rumours it will return because of closures to other tracks, but it is primarily a well-used Flat course. It is a shame that the traditional grandstands, dating to the beginning of last century, have given way to 1970s structures as part of a modernizing scheme, but the replacements are not an eyesore.

The straight course is considered an ideal place to school youngsters and the Prix Djebel and Prix Imprudence at the start of the season are usually France's best Classic trials. July's Prix Robert Papin, for the swiftest of two-year-olds, is the biggest event of the programme and attracts a weekend crowd of a few thousand, while Miesque, who won the Imprudence in 1987 before carrying all before her, has her own eponymous race there.

Another attraction for trainers is that Maisons-Laffitte tends to offer ground that is not too fast. They should be careful what they wish for, though, as it is liable to flooding. When the Seine dramatically burst its banks in 2016, only the trees and white running rails could be seen above the water.

The stables, designed by the great French architect François Mansart, were supposedly a wonder to behold but no longer exist. However, his Château de Maisons-Laffitte still stands and is now a museum and art gallery dedicated to the horse.

RIGHT: The unusual layout of the racecourse means that these stalls could be starting races in either direction.

ABOVE: Newmarket, Maisons-Laffitte and Lexington make up their own twinned cities Triple Crown.

Meydan

Dubai, UAE

If it was the wish of Sheikh Mohammed bin Rashid Al Maktoum, the ruler of Dubai, for Meydan to stand out like a beacon for the emirate's ambition in racing, then he achieved it in at least one sense. His brainchild is simply enormous, dominating the desert horizon looking south of the city, and no less staggering once arriving at its gates.

It is said that Meydan cost at least $1.25 billion to construct. Building work pressed on through various financial crises and continued around the clock before its official opening in 2010.

Racing has only been held formally in Dubai since the early 1990s, driven by Sheikh Mohammed and his extended family's passion for the horse. The site encompasses part of an old and now non-existent racecourse, the more intimate Nad Al Sheba, which was usurped by the bells and whistles of Meydan.

The grandstand itself stakes a claim to be the longest building in the world. Created by the Malaysian architect and polymath Teo Ah Khing it stretches for almost a mile. It has a magnificent, cantilevered crescent roof fitted with solar panels that hovers above facilities catering for 80,000 people and adjoins a five-star trackside hotel with an infinity pool at the top of it. Even the car park was designed in the shape of an emblematic falcon and the Maktoum family have their own private access junction off the nearby motorway.

Given the oppressive heat of the Gulf through much the year, horses work on the track in the early hours of the morning and meetings tend to be scheduled in the cool of the evening. The season fits neatly into the cooler few months and concludes after the Dubai World Cup meeting at the end of March.

There are stables for domestic runners dotted along the back straight and even a separate training circuit for international arrivals still confined under quarantine, such is the level of planning that has gone into this facility.

For many years the most valuable race on the planet, the World Cup, was devised to attract the cream of international middle-distance thoroughbreds to meet on neutral soil. It has succeeded in Dubai but only after some tinkering with the artificial Tapeta racing surface, replaced by dirt in 2015 in order to lure more North American contenders like U.S. Horse of the Year, California Chrome. This mile-and-one-furlong dirt loop sits inside a mile-and-a-half grass circuit which is considered fair for European horses, albeit for those which prefer fast ground.

TOP: A clash of cultures in the Meydan paddock.

ABOVE: Victor Espinoza on California Chrome wins the 2016 Dubai World Cup.

OPPOSITE: Like the World Archipelago in Dubai, Meydan is beautiful even when viewed from a satellite.

jumps, although a tricky downhill slope has to be negotiated. A few British and Irish trainers have been tempted by the prize money but it is suitable only for those few that prefer fast ground. The Irish pairing of Blackstairmountain and Ruby Walsh became the first Europeans to win it when they held on in a driving finish in 2013.

LEFT: Horses being led around the paddock in 2016 during the Satsuki Sho, the Japanese 2000 Guineas.

OPPOSITE: Mirco Demuro celebrates his 500th JRA winner in 2016 and is presented with his very own 'Turfy'.

BELOW AND BELOW LEFT: The largest crowd of the year at Nakayama watches Races 3 and 4 during the 61st Arima Kinen Day on December 25, 2016.

Newmarket

Suffolk, England

All those who work in Newmarket's racing industry and enjoy its two racecourses owe a debt to King Charles II. Exiled to Europe following the death of his father Charles I for the years of Oliver Cromwell's parliamentary rule, he eventually took the throne in 1661.

Charles simply loved this town on the Cambridgeshire/Suffolk border and would visit every spring and summer. The Merry Monarch, so known for his fondness for a good time, would wander down the main street and engage with ordinary folk, an act recorded by politician Sir John Reresby who noted, "he let himself down from Majesty to the very degree of a country gentleman".

The king was passionate about cock-fighting, carousing and horses, and his legacy is essentially the creation of the modern form of organized racing on the vast expanse of heathland. He built houses, stables and founded an event known as the Newmarket Town Plate, riding the winner of the first recorded running in 1671. It is still staged today, the prize being a box of the town's renowned pork sausages.

The Rowley Mile course, named after Charles's hacking horse Old Rowley, is used during the spring and autumn season, and is divided from the summer July Course by the Devil's Dyke, an ancient earthworks. Both have a long and deceptively undulating home straight of at least

a mile, with a right-angled bend for longer races, and share some common ground beyond the reach of the naked eye.

It can feel as if the two courses divide between business and pleasure. The Rowley Mile is often a bleak place at the time of the first Flat meeting in April with its modern Millennium grandstand. It is home to the first two British Classics, the 1,000 and 2,000 Guineas, which usually define

RIGHT: Despite looking flat from up in the stands or on television, Newmarket's Rowley Mile is deceptively undulating in the final stages.

BELOW: Training gallops can be seen to the far right and left of the track.

the career of a champion three-year-old colt or filly. It also stages what are often considered the keynote tests in Britain for promising two-year-olds, the Dewhurst Stakes and the Cheveley Park Stakes. The winners frequently become the winter favourites for the following season's Guineas.

The Rowley Mile has several ridges to overcome and culminates in the Dip, where a downhill penultimate furlong transitions into an uphill final furlong. In 2011, Newmarket showcased the most scintillating performance by the greatest horse of modern times, Frankel, in the 2,000 Guineas. Trained by the town's favourite son, the late Sir Henry Cecil, the colt bounded into the lead leaving the stalls and was an almost inconceivable 15 lengths clear by halfway. He was still half a dozen lengths in front by the line, his sixth win in an unbeaten 14-race career.

The July Course, meanwhile, is host to evening fixtures and popular post-race concerts and its feature three-day July meeting is more like a garden party. The charming old-fashioned stands happily survived the careful recent modernization process and the weighing room has a thatched roof.

Horses are saddled around a pre-parade ring entirely shaded by beech trees in a scene so traditional one could almost imagine Charles II walking in, or at least the nineteenth century's greatest jockey, Fred Archer.

Binoculars and the giant television screen greatly improve viewing, as for the most part the horses are far in the distance, but this is how it has always been. Newmarket's racecourses are informally referred to as 'headquarters' in a nod to the town's position as the unofficial capital of world racing. There are 2,500 horses trained on a network of gallops spreading in different directions, so it is no idle claim to pre-eminence.

It has been managed for nearly three centuries by the Jockey Club and the venerable institution has a beautiful building on the High Street for its members - the Jockey Club Rooms – filled with priceless works by George Stubbs and Sir Alfred Munnings.

Newmarket is also home to Britain's oldest and most prominent equine auctioneer Tattersalls and the majority of the country's finest stud farms are dotted over the surrounding countryside. The National Horseracing Museum, in Palace House, has recently re-opened after a glossy transformation and now includes a sporting art gallery. Fittingly, parts of the building date back to Charles II's day.

Obihiro Racetrack

Hokkaido, Japan

Japan is well known for its cultural curiosities and ban'ei racing can safely be fitted into that category. Draught horses, pulling a sled weighing more than half a tonne, are steered over a 200-metre straight course which includes two hills. It is a traditional sport with its origins in farming from a century or so ago. A few smaller tracks have closed and since 2007 the sport has only taken place at Obihiro, a city in the middle of an agricultural region on the northern island of Hokkaido.

The venue, which opened as a standard racecourse in 1932, is otherwise nondescript and suburban with a golf driving range in the middle. Its ban'ei course is rather more remarkable. Races of eight runners emerge from widened starting stalls and keep to lanes, reaching what could be generously described as a canter before the first bump in this equine BMX track. The first is a metre (3.25 feet) high and usually negotiated comfortably before the horses slow to a walk, or sometimes a stop for a breather, before the second hill of 1.7 metres (5.5 feet).

Riders, wearing jockey silks and perched on the heavy sleds, use long reins to control and encourage their charges. They steel themselves for one big effort up the steeper bank and onwards towards the finish.

Ban'ei is a competition of power rather than speed. Taking place on sand, races usually take a couple of minutes, so the bonus for spectators (and punters) is that they are able to walk alongside their chosen horse and continue urging them on. A photo finish is unlikely, with the winner only called when the back of the sled has crossed the line.

Racing takes place throughout the year at Obihiro, Saturday to Monday, through sunshine and even the snow of this chilly corner of Japan, and it can attract a couple of thousand along. Prize money is lower than for thoroughbred events but horses appear to be able to enjoy longer careers. They are twice the size of racehorses and are generally crosses of French Percheron, Belgian and Breton draughts.

They are bred in Hokkaido and their careers pan out in a similar way, with an established racing programme building from minor events to Grade 1s, where the best mares and stallions can earn themselves a stud career. Unfortunately, the aforementioned breeds are also coveted for their meat, so the fates of some of the other runners might best be left unsaid.

The showpiece race is every March, the Ban'ei Kinen, where the horses must drag a full tonne. Appropriately, it was won on multiple occasions by the mightily-named Super Pegasus and Tomoe Power.

BELOW: Sled racing is a year-round pursuit for the draught horses of Obihiro.

Golden Spike Event Center

Ogden, Utah, America

You would be forgiven for thinking that chariot racing was for tunic-wearing devotees of the film *Ben Hur*, but it's a serious business for a few clubs in the mountain states of north-western America.

It is not so much a Roman sport as a regional one, thought to have been invented in the Wyoming town of Thayne in the 1920s among bored farmers using their milk delivery sleds, or cutters. A world championship was formed there in 1965, which is now held at the Golden Spike Event Center in Ogden, Utah, just north of Salt Lake City.

Nowadays the competitions are predominantly on wheels rather than runners and are strictly regulated in that the driver and his rig, not

BELOW: An evenly matched contest at Ogden. Both chariots are past the finishing line and, though it doesn't look like it, are beginning to slow down into the bend of the old dirt oval.

counting the two horses, must weigh no less than 275lbs (125kgs). The keenest, or those of larger stature, invest in light-weight nylon harnesses and even have chariots made out of magnesium.

The race is much like a drag race for cars, between two drivers over just 440 yards. From start to finish takes only 22 seconds. It is even less of a global championship than Major League Baseball's World Series, as most involved have a family history in the sport and hail from the chariot heartland of Utah, Idaho or Wyoming. It is about far more about prestige and a trophy than the prize money. However, to make it to the final requires qualification from clubs and states through harsh winter weather, and then through heats in different divisions over a couple of weekends at Golden Spike.

Racing takes place on the Weber Downs racetrack, but the well-maintained centre itself has indoor and outdoor arenas for a number of rural pursuits. One can watch such attractions as rodeos, roping horses and sorting cattle.

The racecourse itself, a wide dirt oval, offers a glorious vista of the often snow-capped Wasatch Range on the western edge of the Rocky Mountains. It was once used for conventional racing, but this being ultra-conservative Utah, nearly all forms of gambling are prohibited and use of the track was mired in politics. There have been some attempts to reintroduce American Quarter-Horse racing. These squat and speedy animals have been put to use pulling the chariots and have the advantage that they are considerably cheaper to buy than a thoroughbred horse.

LEFT: The Rocky Mountains which form the backdrop to Ogden's dirt track are often snow-capped, but at Jackson Hole in Wyoming, cutter racing can take place on a snow-packed course.

Hipodromo Argentino de Palermo

Buenos Aires, Argentina

Residents of Buenos Aires are spoiled for choice when it comes to racing. There will be a meeting every day at one of the city's three main venues; Palermo, San Isidro and La Plata, and many more throughout the rest of the country.

San Isidro is capable of holding 100,000 and is the site of Argentina's biggest race, the Gran Premio Carlos Pellegrini, as well as a huge training centre.

However, it is newer and much less interesting than Palermo, which was the first to open in the capital in 1876, and created so much interest that public transport was insufficient for the amount of people that wanted to go. The racecourse is in the chic neighbourhood of Palermo and next to the polo fields which are the mecca of that sport.

By 1908, the original grandstands were ready for a replacement and the design by architect Louis Faure-Dujarric continues to impress to this day. The Frenchman also created Court Philippe Chatrier, the main stadium for the French Open tennis at Roland-Garros, as well as a number of townhouses in Paris, but he let his imagination run away with him at Palermo. The building is in a grandiose, Beaux-Arts style, with gilded features, balustrades, pilasters, columns and statues.

Palermo is best known for its dirt racing and its circuit, a mile and a half long, is one of the largest in the world. The Gran Premio Nacional, or Argentine Derby, each November, is quite a crowd pleaser as the field start right in front of the stands.

The Labour Day holiday on May 1st is traditionally a very important day's racing, when 50,000 or so turn up to see a card including five Group 1 races. As with other South American countries, a major meeting lasts far longer than in Europe and can start at 1pm and continue until 10pm.

Despite its grand appearance, visitors might find Argentinian racing a little more egalitarian than other similar jurisdictions. The general public are allowed into most areas and the best horses are not all owned by a small handful of people as elsewhere.

There is a high standard of racing and jockeyship; Argentina has one of the most productive breeding industries and it is a competitive marketplace with horses exported for decades. Candy Ride won at Palermo in 2002 before going on to perform well in North America.

LEFT: Promising winners of big races in Argentina are often marked for export to North America and Europe.

OPPOSITE TOP: Palermo's main entrance, dating back to 1908, is as striking as any racecourse in the world.

OPPOSITE BOTTOM: More modern racehorse sculptures in front of the main grandstand are something of a departure for traditional Palermo.

Pardubice

Czech Republic

In Britain, the ultimate test of horsemanship and derring-do would lie somewhere between riding around the Grand National at Aintree and the Badminton Horse Trials. In the lowlands towards the centre of the Czech Republic, they have the closest approximation of the two at Pardubice.

Preparing to ride in the Velka Pardubicka must make the hands of even the most experienced jump jockeys slightly clammy, at least until they get over the fourth fence. The Taxis, an enormous hedge obscuring an even more formidable

trench, is jumped only once a year, and that is enough for most.

The Pardubicka is staged over 31 different obstacles over four and a quarter miles. They include water jumps, hedges, ditches and an Irish bank, with ploughed earth replacing turf in some of the sections. Runners proceed at little more than a canter and the layout is so confusing that

BELOW: The attritional Velka Pardubicka is the Everest of steeplechases. In 1909 only three horses started the race and none finished.

newcomers find it wiser just to follow the locals.

It is a race that has attracted international interest since 1874 and George Williamson remains the only jockey to have won both the Pardubicka and the Grand National, from way back in the 1890s. Many other British, German and Italian names are on the roll of honour from that period before the event became hidden behind the iron curtain.

In 1973 Chris Collins became the first Briton to ride in it since the first World War. The thrill-seeking amateur had read about the fearsome race in an article in *Country Life* and returned with tales of Eastern European jockeys attaching themselves by rope so they would not lose their horse and could remount. Collins and his horse Stephen's Society won, paving the way for more riders, and many more foreign spectators.

Pardubice is a wooded racecourse with neat and functional grandstands. It holds Flat racing and

a few qualification meetings for the Pardubicka through the summer. The race day in October is quite informal with the fumes of Czech pilsner and grilled meats heavy in the air.

It is such an esoteric event that it is no surprise that the locals are hard to beat nowadays, and the domestic breeding industry is respected. Course specialists tend to rack up two or three consecutive victories while the undoubted modern day master is the pinched figure of Josef Vana, who won it for the eighth time at the age of 58 in 2011.

As with the fences at Aintree, the steady toll of horse fatalities in the race have compelled the organizers to reduce some of the more fearsome obstacles. Taxis has claimed the lives of 28 horses over the years and though the height remains the same, the ditch on the other side is considerably smaller than when Chris Collins won the race.

OPPOSITE: Josef Bartos riding Sixteen, left, and Jan Korpas on Bremen Plan jump the monster fourth fence, Taxis, during the 121st Velka Pardubicka. The ditch below used to be two metres deep but it has been reduced in recent years to one metre.

BELOW LEFT: Even the most straightforward of obstacles can be a problem for tired horses. Over a quarter of the race is run across ploughed fields.

BELOW AND BOTTOM: The master at work, Czech celebrity Josef Vana who has won the race an incredible eight times, his last victory coming at the age of 58.

Pimlico

Baltimore, America

"Pimlico is more than a dirt track bounded by four streets. It is an accepted American institution, devoted to the best interests of a great sport, graced by time, respected for its honourable past." So said Alfred G. Vanderbilt in words that can hardly be improved upon as to why this racecourse must be considered remarkable.

Vanderbilt, from one of the East Coast's blue-chip families, was a nattily dressed figure who lived the life of Gatsbyesque glamour. He fell in love with racing when taken to Pimlico as a boy and was to own the Baltimore track in the 1930s and 40s, instigating a match race between Seabiscuit and War Admiral in 1938 which the former won by four lengths.

It is said that the racecourse was born of a wager. Oden Bowie, then governor of Maryland, was dining with friends in Saratoga, New York in 1868 and the guests decided to hold a race for their yearling horses, two years hence. The winner of what would be called the Dinner Party

RIGHT: Cloud Computing, on the far side, ridden by Javier Castellano beats Classic Empire ridden by Julien Leparoux to win the 142nd Preakness Stakes.

(now Dixie) Stakes would host the losers and Bowie decided to construct a new track to stage it. Some 12,000 people came to see the race landed by a horse called Preakness, who was then commemorated in his own event, one which has become an institution in American racing.

By 1890, the Maryland Jockey Club had ended its lease on Pimlico because of financial issues and the Preakness moved first to Morris Park (now lost in New York's Bronx) and then Gravesend on Coney Island. The Jockey Club finally got its house in order and reopened Pimlico, and the Preakness came home 20 years later.

W. T. Ryan, the owner of the 1909 winner Effendi, was the first to receive an honour which remains a tradition today. His colours were painted upon a weathervane in the shape of a jockey sitting upon the wooden clubhouse. The Preakness, which had slightly waned in importance thanks to its exile, grew again. It is now the second leg of the American Triple Crown, and the Kentucky Derby winner invariably reappears at the track a fortnight later in the quest for equine immortality. The horse that completes a lap and a third of the one-mile dirt oval the fastest will be covered in a garland of yellow flowers, falsely still described as black-eyed Susans even though it is the wrong season for that plant to bloom.

Pimlico is just behind Saratoga among the country's oldest courses and its clubhouse was in the style of a Victorian hotel, full of priceless racing artwork and records dating back to the very beginning. Calamitously, it burned down in a fire in 1966 and everything was destroyed bar the aforementioned metal weathervane. A replica in the middle of the track is now used to display the winning Preakness silks.

Jacques Kelly, a long-serving local reporter wrote in the *Baltimore Sun* that: "Marylanders, Baltimoreans were very sentimental about the building. Racing had a pretty good comeback in the 1970s as a sport, but I don't think Pimlico as a track ever quite recovered after that."

One major problem has been the evolution of Baltimore, which is one of the most dangerous of American cities, and the setting for the classic crime drama, *The Wire*. Pimlico sits on the perimeter of the crime-ridden north-east suburb of Park Heights. If it was bad enough having an uninspiring view of stable blocks and run-down housing on the back-stretch (pictured left), the foreground is little better with the grandstands badly in need of refurbishment.

The dated facilities are in operation for only a couple of months in late spring and are scarcely populated but for the two days in May around the Preakness. Then, though, 130,000 flock to this otherwise neglected location. Temporary stands are erected but the majority of guests stand in the middle. There is a discernible rise in the infield which was once a popular viewing spot for trainers and owners, giving the course its other nickname 'Old Hilltop'.

Whilst the venue constantly seems to be on the verge of extinction, it remains revered not for its physical beauty, but for the stories of so many racing legends to have visited from Preakness himself and Seabiscuit onwards.

BELOW: The black-eyed Susan is the signature drink of the Preakness Stakes.

Point-to-Point racing

(various, Britain and Ireland)

British and Irish racing is televised around the world these days and millions will already be familiar with Royal Ascot, Cheltenham and the Curragh and the elite jockeys and trainers who take the starring roles.

Fewer will be aware that, for over half of the year, both countries have a separate amateur tier of the sport with as many competitors and even more racecourses.

Point-to-point racing has been intertwined with National Hunt (jump racing), ever since the first match race between Edmund Blake and Cornelius O'Callaghan in County Cork in 1752. The two gentlemen decided to have a contest over the four and a half miles between Buttevant Church and St Mary's Church, Doneraile; jumping hedges and walls along the way. A view of the church steeple ensured that the two riders knew where the finish was, coining the phrases 'steeplechase' and to be racing from 'point to point'.

This early form of the sport was for competitors rather than spectators as they galloped through

stretches of countryside, and it continued in this way until the start of the nineteenth century, when racecourses in circuits more of today's style were appearing. It was not until the early twentieth century that National Hunt racing (known as 'under Rules' and largely for professionals) began to become distinct from point-to-pointing (or racing 'between the flags').

Attending a point-to-point still feels like an authentic experience of the early beginnings of jump racing. Meetings are held in open countryside, there are no grandstands or large television screens and everyone is there for the fun of it. Races are split into particular events for ladies, young horses and some for members of specific hunts. Spectators will often have no idea of the actual runners in each race until they are read out over the loud speaker.

The events are held on weekends from winter through to spring, overlapping with the fox

RIGHT: James O'Connor celebrates after winning a race on Gentle Duke at the Portman Hunt point-to-point held at the Badbury Rings in Dorset.

hunting season, and are organized by local hunt clubs around the regions. A horse can qualify to run at a point-to-point provided it has a certificate to prove it has been out hunting.

There are over 100 purely point-to-point racecourses either side of the Irish Sea, many of which are only used for one day a year before they revert to their natural use. Their variety is one of the greatest attractions; they can range from small muddy fields to the well-groomed grounds of smart country estates and many pass through remarkable scenery.

One of the most popular dates in the diary is in early March at Didmarton, on the Duke

TOP: A fence at the North Shropshire Hunt point-to-point meeting at Eyton On Severn, near Shrewsbury, Shropshire.

RIGHT: Tiverton Staghounds organize point-to-points at Bratton Down in Devon set against the beautiful Exmoor National Park.

of Beaufort's estate in Gloucestershire where the Badminton Horse Trials are held, while traditionalists love Bratton Down, with its ancient turf on the side of a hill at the edge of Exmoor.

One of the grandest of all is Friars Haugh at Kelso in the Scottish Borders, with the imposing turrets of Floors Castle forming a backdrop. They come in all shapes and sizes but common themes are that the fences are slightly smaller than steeplechase races run under Rules and that virtually every race is over three miles.

Some of the Irish tracks have idiosyncratic names, including The Pigeons which is near Athlone, and the particularly appropriate Horse And Jockey at Cashel in County Tipperary. Bellharbour in County Clare (pictured right and below right), where they race between stone walls on the craggy west coast of Ireland, is one of the most picturesque settings you could imagine to watch horse racing.

The idea that point-to-pointing is related to hunting might suggest that it is the exclusive preserve of the landed gentry. Certainly, there are meetings in well-heeled corners of the Cotswolds, Yorkshire and Scotland that have a high count of Range Rover Vogues and gaudily-coloured trousers but in both countries, it is a sport that is embraced by all sections of the rural community. Entrance is usually cheap and there is certainly no dress code.

Meetings serve a variety of purposes. It is a hobby for some, and business for others. Not exactly in terms of prize-money, which is usually only a couple of hundred pounds for the winner, but as a launchpad for a professional career. Many of today's top professional jump jockeys cut their teeth in point-to-points, while young horses that could go on to win a Cheltenham Gold Cup – including three-times winner Best Mate – can take their first tentative steps on one of these rural racecourses.

ABOVE: One of the perks of being a steward at this Herefordshire point-to-point meeting is four feet of elevation and complementary straw bales for ascending their lofty position.

TOP and RIGHT: The glorious Bellharbour point-to-point course.

In Ireland, where most of the best jumps horses are bred and licensed professional trainers are allowed to have runners, they are used as a shop window and most runners are for sale. There are many stories of horses winning an Irish point in impressive fashion when a gullible wealthy British owner happened to be on the scene and the trainer could virtually name their price.

There will be at least a few hundred spectators at every meeting, whatever the weather. There are often chances to see old equine friends, as some familiar horses from National Hunt racing drop back to points at the ends of their career. The sport received a notable publicity boost when Victoria Pendleton, the Olympic gold medal-winning cyclist, took up point-to-pointing in 2015 with the aim of qualifying for a race for amateur riders at the Cheltenham Festival. She would eventually come fifth in the Foxhunter Chase at Cheltenham in 2016 and won her first race at Wincanton riding a 5–4 favourite, Pacha Du Polder.

ABOVE: The Duke of Buccleuch's point-to-point at Friars Haugh skirts the river Tweed with Floors Castle in the background.

ABOVE LEFT: Victoria Pendleton riding According to Sarah in the Ladies Open race during the Barbury Castle point-to-point, near Marlborough, in December 2015.

LEFT: A tightly packed field clear the last fence at the Duke of Beaufort's Hunt point-to-point in Gloucestershire.

Pompadour

Correze, France

Pompadour is not one of the major French racecourses but it outranks many in terms of history and even beauty. For a start, there is a château with its roots dating back to the times of Richard The Lionheart looking over the end of the home straight. The fifteenth century gaff was once bought by Louis XV and given to his famous mistress, Jeanne Antoinette Poisson, or Madame de Pompadour, in 1745. While there was damage and some demolition in the late eighteenth century, what remains is a majestic building in a pinkish grey hue, with a moat and unusual, pointed pepperpot towers.

The racecourse, which was twinned first with the now closed-down Folkestone and subsequently the pretty East Sussex track of Plumpton, has been in operation since 1837. It is well-supported by the folk around Limoges and Brive in this rural part of central France. Whilst the Limousin region is famed for its cattle, it is also horse country and the Pompadour National Stud, founded by Louis XV, is neighbour to the château. It is reputed to have bred the finest riding horses for the cavalry and is the primary breeding centre of the Anglo-Arabian horse.

There is a mile-and-a-quarter sand track for Flat racing in a pear-shape, but it is better known for its jump courses, which are spread in a

higgledy-piggledy fashion across the undulating middle of the field, with a range of hurdles and steeplechase fences as well banks, oxers and live hedges. There are around a dozen mixed meetings per year, mainly on Sundays in July and August, as well as horse shows featuring other equestrian disciplines.

France's best jump trainers and jockeys, including Guillaume Macaire and Jacques Ricou, have made regular appearances and the course is often viewed as a good trialling ground before a horse runs in a more valuable race at Pau in the south-west, or Auteuil in Paris. Empereur River was a frequent visitor and was even a rare French runner in the Grand National at Aintree, admittedly running true to his 250-1 odds.

The big names always come down for the Prix Basile et Bernard Lachaud Grand Cross in the middle of August, a cross-country event over more than three miles of the difficult terrain worth an impressive €45,000.

LEFT: The disjointed nature of the jumps course at Pompadour means loose horses find it harder to keep up the chase.

RIGHT and TOP RIGHT: Unusually, jump racing takes place over different sections of grass followed by a sandy run past the stands.

Pukekohe Park

Auckland, New Zealand

Many racecourses are used for other sporting events but it is remarkable to find one in the middle of a motor racing circuit.

Pukekohe Park stages a dozen race meetings but is better-known nationally for the racing on wheels rather than four legs, as it was a regular venue for the New Zealand Grand Prix. This was never part of the Formula One World Championship, but has been attached to a variety of motorsport formulae over the years. Even so, the likes of Graham Hill, Jack Brabham and Jackie Stewart competed there in the Tasman Series in the 1960s.

It brings back memories of a similar venture in England, when Aintree was known not only as the home of the Grand National, but on five occasions hosted the British Grand Prix.

Although Pukekohe Park Raceway is no longer the Kiwi petrolhead destination it was, it has not declined to the extent of Liverpool, which now holds motorsport events in a very limited form. The speedy 2.82 kilometres (1.8 mi) Pukekohe circuit is used for various national and club-level races for classic and touring cars as well as regular testing days.

The racecourse, which opened in 1919, came much earlier. The car circuit was only added in 1963, to replace Ardmore Aerodrome as home of the Grand Prix.

Most peculiarly, the car circuit and racecourse share a large main grandstand and other spectator facilities, with the road winding all the way outside a simple grass oval which, at nearly a mile and two furlongs, is the second-longest in New Zealand.

It is a huge space that can cater for music festivals, with all-weather and training circuits within the racing surface and stabling facilities for 190 horses as well as an apprentice jockey school.

There are 65 licenced racecourses in New Zealand, some of which are very provincial, but Pukekohe's position just half an hour from Auckland ensures the presence of many of the sport's top competitors. It has an important day each November with several Group 2 races headed by the Counties Cup.

Punchestown

Kildare, Ireland

Irish racing has always maintained a strong link with rural communities and nowhere is this more apparent than at the country's premier jumping venue.

Punchestown was originally used by the local Kildare Hunt for its race meetings through open countryside, with an event recorded as early as 1824. It had been chosen as its permanent home by 1850. The land was bequeathed to the hunt many years ago by the La Touche family and Punchestown still belongs to it today. The fox on the racecourse's logo is something of a giveaway and the hunt's red-jacketed members regularly patrol the course at fixtures.

Racing proved popular and the hunt ball inside the town hall of nearby Naas was supposed to be an especially lavish occasion, drawing crowds of onlookers. The meeting attracted Royal interest in 1868 from a 27-year-old Prince Of Wales, later King Edward VII, and it is reckoned that 150,000 turned up.

Coming only a year after the Fenian Rising against British rule, the Prince's attendance concerned his mother, Queen Victoria, who wrote: "I much regret that the occasion chosen should be the races as it naturally strengthens the belief, already too prevalent, that your chief object is amusement." The Prince, who was well known for his love of drinking, gambling, shooting and especially the turf, quickly replied: "I am very anxious, dear Mama, that you should fully understand that I do not go there at all for my amusement, but as a duty."

It was perhaps the association with such a British aristocratic pursuit that led Sinn Fein to targeting the hunts in 1919 during the Irish War of Independence. In retaliation, Punchestown decided to cancel its race meeting, and the stand-off continued the following year.

The modern-day Punchestown Festival in late April brings in 100,000 people to Kildare across five days and is Ireland's foremost jumps meeting, usually the final start of the campaign for Cheltenham and Aintree heroes in the equivalent versions of the Gold Cup and Champion Hurdle.

This well-developed facility sits in ancient countryside as the eye can see, rolling into the Wicklow Mountains beyond and there is a menhir (standing stone) known as the Punchestown Longstone just outside the gates.

A link with the more recent past is maintained by what is known as 'the banks', a cross-country course snaking over a variety of obstacles which is used a few times a year. "There was a hurdles course but all the steeplechase races were over the banks and stone walls," explained Charles O'Reilly, a Punchestown board and Hunt Club member. "It was only in 1960 that brush fences were introduced and it was a subject of great controversy. It divided the hunt committee down the middle."

The track is square and over two miles in length, with inviting steeplechase fences and a long climb to the finish; whilst the hurdles course on the inside is considered much sharper.

Meanwhile, the banks course is a little different to what it was and includes an obstacle adjoining a replica of the Glendalough monastery, created for the 1991 European Eventing Championship which was held on the land. One of the races it is used for at the Festival is the Bishopscourt Cup, contested for a trifling sum and anachronistically restricted to horses owned by legitimate farmers upon whose land the Kildare Hunt crosses during its season. Needless to say, it is of the utmost importance to those involved.

The La Touche Cup is the other great prize over this unusual assault course and was the playground of Risk Of Thunder, who was owned by the actor Sean Connery and won it an incredible seven times from 1995. As well as farmers, the church has long had a link with Punchestown. Charles O'Reilly recalled

even going hunting with priests but there was a time, under the directive of a particularly condemnatory Archbishop of Dublin, when they were banned from going racing. Ignoring this ecumenical matter, members of the clergy watched covertly from a mound on the back straight known as 'Priest's Hill', with youths relaying their bets back to the course bookmakers.

Punchestown received a £9 million redevelopment in 1998 and much of its architecture is in fitting grey stone, with a courtyard complex housing the paddock. It has other good jump meetings through the year, including December's John Durkan Memorial Chase and its vast space has enabled it to host other attractions including the Oxegen music festival and a concert by the Irish band U2.

ABOVE LEFT: Steep banks can easily take horse and rider out of their rhythm.

LEFT: Racegoers Niamh Lawler (left) and Katie Ann Ging, ask for tips from Sean Maher, from Templemore, County Tipperary, who has attended the Punchestown Festival for more than 60 years.

TOP: Rarely has an important meeting gone by in recent years without a Ruby Walsh-ridden winner.

TOP RIGHT: For those who failed to bring binoculars, help is at hand at Punchestown.

ABOVE: Sections of the banks course have been used for three-day eventing competitions.

when it became the first horse to win races on all three consecutive weekends. He returned the following year for an unsuccessful attempt at the White Turf's most valuable contest, the Group 2 Grosser Preis Von St Moritz. Even Frankie Dettori has made an appearance and was treated like royalty in 2010, arriving at the track in a Rolls Royce before being besieged by the media and autograph hunters. The multiple champion jockey quickly satisfied his adoring audience by riding the winner of the opening race.

The racing at St. Moritz is not without danger. The White Turf has suffered bad publicity with accidents after horses have fallen over in recent years and some criticism has been aimed at its safety management. A crack in the ice discovered in the 2017 meeting caused a day of the meeting to be abandoned and, as with the long-term future of all winter sports in the Alps, the effects of global warming could be felt keenly in time.

LEFT TOP: Racing on the White Turf would be impossible without specially adapted horseshoes for the runners.

ABOVE: Far from being a modern innovation, there has been racing at St. Moritz since 1906, although nowadays the quality of horses is far greater.

OPPOSITE: Guyon Maxime riding Take a Guess (centre) leads the pack in the GP Longines race in 2017. Racing was later suspended after jockey George Baker was injured in a bad fall.

San Siro

Milan, Italy

Italian racing has been in dire straits for many years, so much so that in 2014 the authorities owed such a backlog of outstanding prize money that the European Pattern Committee decided that its important races would no longer be recognized at international standard. Horses were sold overseas and the entire breeding industry appeared in jeopardy.

The sport does continue but its decline and poor governance has saddened the nation's enthusiasts, especially as it has a rich history and some fine racecourses, including Pisa and the Capanelle in Rome.

Ranking as high as any is the Ippodromo del Galoppo at San Siro in Milan, with its grandstands dating from 1920, although many who live in this quiet north-western district of the city might be unaware it exists. The name San Siro is associated with the football stadium, home to Italian giants AC Milan and Internazionale. It was redesigned for the 1990 World Cup and towers above the racecourse next door.

There has been racing at San Siro since 1888 but it was decided in 1911 to completely redesign

the racecourse. Architect Vietti Violi's design, which took a few years to come to fruition, features neoclassical grandstands and a beautiful old weighing room. It is thought that 25,000 came to the opening meeting.

The writer Ernest Hemingway visited in 1918 with his companion Agnes von Kurowsky and did not paint the sport in the most flattering light, claiming to have placed bets on fixed races. San Siro appears in a chapter of Hemingway's *A Farewell To Arms*, when Catherine spots a champion horse that has been disguised as another by being dyed a different colour.

Two of Italy's greatest champions, Nearco and Ribot, both raced at San Siro and, despite the administrative issues, horses and riders still come from across Europe for its big races, mostly held on Sundays through the summer and autumn.

ABOVE RIGHT: Like most departments in Italian racing, San Siro would welcome some more investment in the crumbling facilities.

RIGHT: The gift of 'Leonardo's Horse' did not meet with universal approval.

The greatest attractions are the Italian Oaks, Gran Premio di Milano, Gran Premio del Jockey Club and Premio Federico Tesio, named after the godfather of the Italian breeding industry. Arguably the world's most famous jockey, Frankie Dettori, was born in the city and had his first ride on a pony at San Siro, aged nine.

As the racecourse is only five kilometres from the centre of Milan, it is a surprisingly rural place, surrounded by trees, with a wide, oval-shaped grass course and hedges, with various jumping tracks in the middle. Just across the road at Trenno Park, there is a large training centre and it seems odd that there is an entire community involved within a sport about which most of the Milanese population seems largely oblivious.

Tourists might be more attracted by one of the racecourse's artworks, rather than the racing. Standing in a square outside the entrance to the second grandstands is *Leonardo's Horse*, an enormous bronze statue that was intended to be the work of Leonardo da Vinci himself when he was commissioned by Duke Ludovico Sforza in 1482, but was never created.

An American pilot, Charles Dent, read about it in the late 1970s and became obsessed with bringing the project to life. After spending an inordinate amount of time, and millions of dollars on it, the 24-foot (7.3 metres) creation by sculptor Nina Akamu arrived in parts to be donated to the city of Milan. The racecourse was chosen as its resting place, although reaction was mixed among the art world, as it so often is with reproductions.

ABOVE: The entrance to San Siro is barely noticed by most of Milan's population.

RIGHT: Brilliant jockeys, including Frankie Dettori, have taken their first tentative steps on this track.

185

Santa Anita

California, USA

It does not take long to realise why racing professionals and enthusiasts are so delighted whenever Santa Anita is announced as the host of the peripatetic Breeders' Cup world championships. To be up watching racehorses exercising as the sun rises over the San Gabriel Mountains is one of those life-affirming experiences, especially as the weather usually remains pleasant in early November.

The original track was in another nearby part of Arcadia, now a smart suburb of Los Angeles, and was opened by the pioneering property speculator Elias J. "Lucky" Baldwin in 1907. It was moved to its present site in 1934, funded by a group including film producer Hal Roach and dentist Dr. Charles H. Strub.

Partly due to its proximity to Hollywood, it became a glamorous destination over the next few decades; Frank Sinatra, Bing Crosby and Clark Gable were regulars and even Charlie Chaplin was pictured there.

The first most notable competitor on the track was Seabiscuit, the initially hopeless equine hero of the Great Depression who is depicted by a statue in the parade ring. He ran there 11 times in all but was unsuccessful in his first two attempts at the Santa Anita Handicap, which was staged for $125,000, an enormous amount by anyone's standards.

Tens of thousands were drawn through the gates to see his rather unfortunate defeats in 1937 and 1938 and the triumph on what was to be his final outing in 1940. Scenes for the Oscar-nominated 2003 film adaptation *Seabiscuit* were also filmed at the course.

At the 1984 Los Angeles Olympics, Santa Anita's stabling facilities ensured it was the obvious choice to stage the equestrian events and the Santa Anita Handicap has continued to draw some of America's most famous horses, from Affirmed and John Henry to Game On Dude.

In America, all racecourses are laid out the same, much like supermarkets, independent of location. They have flat, anti-clockwise dirt ovals of around a mile in circumference, but Santa Anita has one particularly unusual feature. There is a separate six-and-a-half-furlong grass sprint course which starts with a downhill section and leads into a right-hand turn, unique for American racing, and one which often takes horses outside their comfort zone. The turf was relaid with a more robust blend of grass in 2016 to cope with an extended fixture list and was described as being like the Augusta National Golf Club by one impressed jockey.

The Hollywood glitterati do not appear with such regularity nowadays but the executive tried to ensure the place retains some of that timeless charm amid a $15 million makeover in 2013, including the Chandelier Room with its spiral staircases and original light fittings and the antique, wood-panelled Director's Room. Some of the magnificent Art Deco building work remains today, including the elegant facade at the entrance to the main grandstand in the Santa Anita livery of mint and pale yellow.

Clockers Corner, the cafe at the top of the home straight, is the spot where jockeys and associated horse-folk go about their daily business. However, anyone is welcome to soak up the early rays amid the palm trees and the sound of galloping hooves. A breakfast option including scrambled eggs, avocado and tomato has even been named after Bob Baffert, the silver-haired Hall of Fame trainer.

BELOW: Santa Anita and Churchill Downs have been the most frequently selected home for the annual Breeders' Cup.

Club Hipico de Santiago

Chile

Chile's premier racecourse must be considered another strong contender in the category of world's most beautiful. It has many virtues, starting with its prime location in the Barrio Republica, an Art Nouveau-inspired neighbourhood of universities and museums, right in the heart of the capital.

The racecourse also boasts the backdrop of the Andes mountains and sits next door to O'Higgins Park, the second largest in Santiago. However, it is its architecture that sets it apart. The British brought the sport of racing to Chile in the nineteenth century but the architectural influence, like much of the surrounding area, derives from France.

Designed by French architect Lucien Henault, its first meeting took place in 1870 and, according to the book *Racecourse Architecture*, by Paul Roberts and Isabelle Taylor, the original iron-framed buildings were in use until 1918. Then began the construction of the marvellous facilities that remain today. The Chilean Josué Smith Solar was brought in for the design, which mimics that of Longchamp.

It took nine years to finish everything, with three grandstands, fountains, a clubhouse and formal gardens. The members' stand is the most like a Parisian track and is an impressive 121m long, divided by four towers and with arched windows and balconies. Smith went further, though, covering almost every wall with Italianate reliefs. Inside are more intricate creations in marble and dark woods.

The two public stands are simpler, and thought to be more influenced by Tuscany with their roofed towers, while the paddock at the back is in a Spanish Revival style.

Santiago is one of three significant racecourses in the country, along with Hipodromo Chile at Independencia on the outskirts of Santiago and Valparaiso Sporting Club in Vina del Mar. It has its share of the important events and has the longest established in Chile, the Premio El Ensayo, 'the test'. It is a race thought to be one of the very oldest in the Americas, worth around £65,000 to the winner, and the stands are full to see it in early November.

Horses tend to belong to the large-scale breeders and ownership still seems to be a largely aristocratic pursuit. Racing in Chile has not been immune to problems but it remains in fairly robust health, with around 2,000 horses in training. Chilean breeders have habitually preferred to import stallions from Europe and North America but their offspring have regularly been exported back and are respected for being tough and hardy types. Cougar II started racing in Chile in the late 60s and later became American Champion Male Turf Horse of 1972.

Unusually for South or North America, Santiago has also followed the example of Longchamp by racing clockwise on a traditionally wide grass circuit of a mile and a half. Meetings are all year round, mostly on Fridays but also Mondays and Sundays and as the turf was becoming so difficult to maintain from frequent use, a sand track was added in the middle.

Visitors had better be prepared for a marathon session though; it is not uncommon for there to be 19 races on the card.

RIGHT: With marathon cards stretching to 19 races, it is little surprise that most racegoers do not attend for the duration.

BELOW: As the then and now images suggest, little has changed at this racecourse in a century, not even the water pressure.

Saratoga

New York State, America

Venerable is the most appropriate word to describe Saratoga, the fondly regarded grandfather of American racecourses. It sits in a leafy, desirable spa town in upstate New York near the Adirondack Mountains and is home to artists, museums and the mineral springs which brought people there in the first place.

Come August, it becomes the centre of the national racing scene and many outsiders arrive to watch America's oldest major race from the most continually used grandstand of any sport in the country.

The building was not present in Saratoga's earliest days (trotting took place in the area now used as a training track as early as 1847) nor at the time of the formal opening in 1863. Nor was it built under the tenure of gang-member-turned-politician John Morrissey which lasted 30 years. It was the subsequent owner, Gottfried "Dutch Fred" Walbaum, an infamous gambler, who realigned the track and built the grandstand which still stands today.

Herbert Langford Warren's design is almost 200 feet (60 metres) long and its most famous feature is a Queen Anne-style slate roof with groups of slanted turrets, held up by wooden trusses. It was painstakingly split into sections to accommodate more spectators in 1902. A rectangular clubhouse a was added in 1928 and grandstand addition (1965) are pleasant but only emphasize, rather than augment, the majesty of the earlier buildings.

Travers Stakes day is full of tradition and the race often draws winners of the Kentucky Derby, Preakness and Belmont Stakes. However, it has been the scene of some famous upsets, such as when 100-1 chance Jim Dandy beat the Triple Crown hero Gallant Fox in 1930, and it has acquired the nickname of the "Graveyard of Champions". In 2015, Keen Ice brought to an end American Pharoah's similarly prolific spree. Greats like Man o'War and Secretariat suffered unexpected defeats in other races on the track.

The Whitney Stakes holds similar prestige as a race for older horses and has featured gallant weight-carrying performers by battlers such as Kelso and Discovery.

The course cannot hold races over exactly a mile, as a starting point joining the bend after the winning line called the Wilson Mile Chute was dismantled in 1971. The dirt oval is nine furlongs, a little longer than the majority of American circuits, and surrounds two turf courses. The inside track is lined by hedges and sometimes stages jump races, although the steeplechase fences used for races like the New York Turf Writers Cup would be classed as hurdles in European parlance.

Saratoga has a few quaint customs and features. The Travers winner receives a huge garland of red carnations and the winning colours are painted on a canoe on a lake in the infield. An unprecedented dead-heat between Alpha and Golden Ticket in 2012 meant that two boats had

to be launched back in the water. A bell is rung by hand exactly 17 minutes before each race to remind jockeys and trainers and, unusually, horses are led to the paddock right through the crowds, allowing great views for the public.

As with other fine American sporting institutions, this one is treated augustly. The lack of air conditioning, the cramped and uncomfortable seating and the attendants in the rest rooms are all considered part of the Saratoga experience.

OPPOSITE: Mike Smith keeps his silks mud-free on the inside rails as he cuts the corner on the turn for home and victory in the 2017 Travers Stakes.

BELOW: The venerable amalgam of grandstands that is the horse racing time capsule of Saratoga.

Lets Run Park

Seoul, South Korea

South Korea is considered one of the most exciting emerging racing nations. Although there is a history of events taking place in the early twentieth century, the capital's racecourse is the oldest of the country's three tracks – and it was only opened in 1989.

The previous site at Ttukseom, home to the city's racing for 36 years, remains an open space but is emblematic of a more closed era in South Korean history when horses were state owned and there was no prize money. There was at least wagering, with racing being one of the only pastimes which the population was allowed to bet on.

Seoul Race Park, to use its more prosaic title, took over on the site dedicated to the equestrian disciplines at the 1988 Olympics. In a southern suburb, easily accessible by public transport, it races every Saturday and Sunday on two anti-clockwise, deep sand ovals. Particularly eye-catching are the size of the two interlinked grandstands, 'Happyville' and 'Luckyville', which take up the entire two-furlong home straight and can hold 80,000 spectators with a baffling array of restaurants and even a lounge on the fifth floor exclusively for foreign visitors.

The South Korean breeding industry is centred on the volcanic island province of Jeju. American stallions were acquired during the 1980s as they were considered to have more suitable bloodlines for the local dirt surfaces. Their offspring have ensured that the standard of horse has increased considerably. Itinerant foreign trainers and jockeys were recruited to stimulate domestic talent, including the British rider Darryll Holland.

Even with only a few fixtures per week, the annual gambling turnover is a staggering $7 billion. Speaking at the Asian Racing Conference in 2014, the Korean Racing Authority's international manager Dr. Seungho Ryu outlined that it was the seventh highest in the world, and the proceeds have allowed average prize money to rank third. Quite an achievement considering when and where they began.

The KRA has aligned itself with the global regulatory framework and 2016 provided two landmark moments. The country had two runners at the Dubai Carnival, with Korean-bred Success Story leading for a long way and eventually finishing third at Meydan behind the subsequent World Cup winner California Chrome.

Then in September, Seoul held its first international meeting and two valuable events attracted runners from seven overseas nations, including England, Ireland and France. Japan took the Korea Cup and the experienced Hong Kong runner Super Jockey won the Korea Sprint. Local runner Macheon Bolt was an encouraging second. As the Cup, sponsored by the American horse sales company Keeneland, was worth £700,000, it is hoped that more tourists will be keen on getting in on the action in future years.

TOP: Lee Hae Dong riding Last Jackpot takes the lead in Race 5 of the 2017 Korean Autumn Racing Carnival.

ABOVE RIGHT: Graceful Leap wins the 2017 Keeneland Korea Sprint.

RIGHT: The parade ring at Lets Run Park.

OPPOSITE: Similar to Sha Tin in Hong Kong, Seoul has a massive LED screen at the finishing post relaying the race to punters in 'Happyville' and 'Luckyville'.

Il Palio

Siena, Italy

Many will describe an annual visit to Cheltenham or Flemington as akin to a religious experience. Around the medieval square of the Piazza del Campo in Siena, racing generates a fervour that is on a whole different level.

On July 2 and August 16 each year, 80,000 cram into the square to witness a colourful and treacherous battle which has been waged since the seventeenth century. Ten jockeys in traditional colours, riding bareback without a saddle or irons and wielding old-fashioned whips, will complete three laps of a clay track on the sloping perimeter. It is a no-holds-barred race and there is no prize money on offer. Riders race for the honour of their contrada or district. In Siena a resident's strongest allegiance is to their contrada, their city comes only a distant second, and their country third.

Before any racing begins, human and equine competitors are taken into local churches for a blessing. One of the races each year is held in honour of the Virgin Mary – the Madonna of Provenzano – the other for a holy shrine in the Tuscan city. The 10 horses and jockeys are not competing individually but for their contrada of which there are 17. Each has their own racing silks and a draw is made to decide which ones will take part in the race.

Tickets for the temporary stands are expensive, selling out well in advance, and only the luckiest can watch from the floors of the surrounding buildings. Most people have to take their chance in the middle, and must arrive hours before the

LEFT: The Palio di Siena is nowhere near as ancient as the Palio di Asti which dates back to 1275. Children in medieval costume take part in a historical parade around the race track at Asti ahead of the race which is held each September.

BELOW: Horses are held behind a thick, winch-tightened rope which is dropped at the start of the race.

OPPOSITE: Extensive safety measures have been brought in to reduce injuries to both horses and riders.

main event to make sure they get a spot. The race itself takes just 75 seconds.

A colourful parade of ancient costumes precedes the race and it is a scene so vivid it was used in the James Bond film *Quantum of Solace*. While the pageantry will enchant the day-tripper, the event is full of rituals beyond the comprehension of the uninitiated. For a native, the race is essentially about local bragging rights for which

preparation goes on all year, and it is a very serious business.

Cosima Spender's revealing 2015 documentary *Palio* focused on the rivalry between Luigi Bruschelli, the most successful current jockey, and the up-and-coming Giovanni Atzeni, cousin of leading British-based rider Andrea. As it investigated their stories, it revealed some of the less savoury aspects of the race. The jockeys

OPPOSITE: Before the horses are unleashed for the real thing, they get to ride a trial race to test out the surface and turns. This is not full speed.

BELOW RIGHT: A member of the 'Contrada of Lupa' celebrates after winning the Palio of the Madonna in 2016. For many the outburst of pride and joy at winning the race is overwhelming.

BELOW: Though the object is to win the race, many competitors have secondary objectives of preventing their great rivals from winning.

and trainers do not identify with a contrada, but simply offer their services and it is said that many thousands of pounds change hands, so important is civic pride.

Machinations, wheeling and dealing continue even to the starting line and it can take some minutes before they have settled into positions in front of the tape. Riders might try to take out others, or perhaps even deliberately let them past.

Once they race, it is not for the faint-hearted. Horses bump, seem to veer almost into the crowd, and jockeys are regularly sent spiralling into the dirt. As soon as the first passes the line, a shot is fired and the winner is immediately surrounded by a mass of jubilant members carrying banners and wearing their uniform. A horse is allowed to be called the winner if it passed the line first without a jockey, provided it is still carrying the contrada colours. Further customs are carried out, followed by a celebratory dinner.

Those of some districts will be almost as delighted by their enemies being unsuccessful as by winning themselves, even if this was achieved by foul play. It is as dangerous as it looks, with regular injuries to horses and riders. Organizers of the Palio have had to bow to legitimate welfare concerns and the horses, which are not thoroughbreds, are specially trained, registered and vetted. But the race is so ingrained in the culture and the people of Siena, it seems sure to remain in some shape or form for many more centuries to come.

Sha Tin

Hong Kong

Hong Kong's premier racecourse is the product of the astounding creation of space in the cramped former British colony. This part of the New Territories which stretches up to the mainland Chinese border, used to be a largely agricultural area on the floodplain of the Shing Mung River. It was developed into a town in the 1970s through an intensive land reclamation project and a channel of the river flows behind the back straight of the racecourse, which was opened in 1978 by the governor of Hong Kong.

What is most remarkable about Sha Tin, which had a second grandstand added in 1985, is that it still looks like an over-ambitious artist's impression in a flashy architecture manual. But one that has been brought to reality. The mountain peaks of the Lion Rock Country Park loom in the background and in the centre of the track is Penfold Park, a landscaped recreational area which even provides a habitat for wild egrets. By the winning post is an LED screen for betting and race replays which is 230 feet (70 metres) long, wider than the wingspan of a Boeing 747.

The grandstands are colossal, capable of accommodating 80,000 people with an overhead walkway linking to a dedicated racecourse station. A vast bank of open-air seating leads up to tiers of restaurants and corporate boxes. Even more impressive is the parade ring behind, with the world's first retractable roof over a paddock which was unveiled in 2004. Again, it allows thousands of race fans to see the horses in the flesh.

Sha Tin tends to hold its meetings on Saturdays and Sundays and while it does not have the cult following of its older sister track, Happy Valley, it is home to all the important races. April's prestigious Queen Elizabeth Cup meeting attracts overseas horses but this is dwarfed by the international meeting in December, which describes itself as the 'Turf World Championships'. The four invitational events, the Cup, Mile, Sprint and Vase, regularly attract the cream of Europe at the end of a long season.

The home team has historically been strongest in the speed department and the likes of Fairy King Prawn and Silent Witness, who both won the Hong Kong Sprint, became particularly popular. The latter went unbeaten in his first 17 starts, all at Sha Tin, up to 2005. All of Hong Kong's horses, usually a number just over 1000, are imported and stabled at Sha Tin but it is possible that this will change in the future following the announcement of a new training centre in Conghua, mainland China.

The facilities came in handy for the equestrian section of the 2008 Olympics, even though it was 1200 miles from Beijing. It was felt Hong Kong was better placed to deal with stabling and quarantine and was freer from diseases. Sha Tin was the first place to receive the Olympic flame.

TOP RIGHT: Sha Tin's parade ring has a retractable roof.

MIDDLE RIGHT: The winning post dressed for the Group 1 Chairman's Sprint Prize.

RIGHT: Aerovelocity parades for the last time at Sha Tin.

LEFT: Like Happy Valley on Hong Kong island, the course is crammed between tower blocks.

Vincennes

Paris, France

For devotees of trotting, a visit to this enormous racecourse on the eastern edge of Paris is *de rigeur*. The sport is not as widespread around the world as thoroughbred horseracing, but has a huge following, particularly in France and Sweden. There are nuances which take a little while to get to grips with, trotting (also known as harness racing) takes place with a light-weight cart called a sulky.

Horses can be disqualified for various violations. The chief foul is if they break out of their stride and into a canter. A trotter will move its legs in diagonal pairs but there is also a variant called pacing, where the horse moves its front and hind legs laterally. That discipline continues

in Australasia, North America and Britain, but trotting is by far the better-known of the two.

Trotting can be traced back to the Netherlands in the sixteenth century and its history in France began in Brittany in 1836. Most of the modern horses are known as Standardbreds, a stockier, high-stepping version of the thoroughbred which was developed in America, although there are still many French and Russian-bred trotters.

The sport was first staged at Vincennes in 1879, which had opened for jump racing six years earlier. It became exclusively a trotting facility in 1934. The racecourse is surrounded by woodland on the southern corner of the Bois de Vincennes public park, which it shares with a zoo, various sporting facilities and an impressive fourteenth century castle.

Facilities have been upgraded with the grandstand redeveloped in 1983. The grey cinder track is vast, with a main outside oval of a mile and a quarter and a shorter inner loop for floodlit night fixtures. Drivers swarm across it like a shoal of sardines as they warm up their horses ahead of a moving start.

Vincennes now holds more than 150 meetings per year, with many on Tuesday or Friday evenings, but the moment the entire trotting community stops is on the last Sunday afternoon in January.

The Prix d'Amerique, worth €1 million and run over a mile and three-quarters, is the most important trotting event in the world. It features the 18 best horses from Europe and sometimes even representatives from across the Atlantic. Vincennes is packed to the rafters with an excitable crowd of more than 30,000, many with flags and painted faces in the colours of particular runners. The race was created in 1920 and named in honour of the American forces whose decisive intervention in the last eight months of the First World War helped achieve an Allied victory.

Watched around the world, the Prix d'Amerique is similar to the Grand National or Melbourne Cup in that it is the one race the general French public might have a bet on. Quite why trotting appeals more to French punters is not quite certain, but one possible reason is that the horses can race for longer, and more frequently, than their thoroughbred cousins, so they become more familiar.

Ourasi was perhaps the greatest French trotter and many of his 50 consecutive victories came at Vincennes. He was the first to claim the Prix d'Amerique four times, the last at the age of 10 in 1990.

The Italian stallion Varenne, nicknamed Il Capitano, had an extraordinary following and in 2001 completed the rarely achieved feat of

taking the Amerique as well as the other grand slam events of the Elitloppet in Stockholm and the Gran Premio della Lotteria in Naples. That year, Varenne also broke the world record of a mile in just over 1 minute and 51 seconds in the Breeders Crown in America.

ABOVE: The combination of rain and a cinder track at Vincennes can make identification and race commentating a nightmare.

RIGHT: From the nation that donated *Liberty Enlightening the World* for New York harbour, an explosion of flag-waving ahead of the Prix d'Amerique in January 2017.

OPPOSITE: French jockey Franck Nivard wins the 97th Prix d'Amerique with the fittingly named Bold Eagle.

Waregem

West Flanders, Belgium

The Belgian racing scene, like its space programme, is not big. It has only two racecourses that are in reasonably regular use – Mons in French Wallonia and one at the seaside city of Ostend, both offering only a moderate standard of racing and prize money.

The town of Waregem has much medieval history and lies close to the French border, 50 miles to the west of Brussels. In an area that saw horrifying action in the First World War, Waregem is also home to the Flanders Field American Cemetery and Memorial.

On one day a year, the Gaverbeek Hippodrome in Waregem hosts a jumps meeting which includes a race that was once among the most important in Europe. The Grand Steeplechase of Flanders was first held in 1858 and, on the first Tuesday in September, it would attract British and French runners. The race was considered on a par with the Grand National.

It was a fearsome event, with the most daunting obstacle being a water jump 5 yards (4.5 metres) wide in front of the stands called the Gaverbeek. In 1861, three brothers from the aristocratic Belgian Roy de Blicquy family all fell simultaneously when jumping it.

Animal welfare issues have led to the Gaverbeek and the enormous ditches no longer featuring in this three-mile race, but it has evolved into a cross-country event with hedges to brush through and a tricky bank to climb. Horses will cover almost three circuits of a winding track around the outside of a trotting oval, deviating temporarily out of view into the countryside.

Even if there is clearly little appetite for regular national racing, the Belgians continue to appreciate the Grand Steeplechase and Waregem's new and permanent grandstand is joined by a temporary city of marquees to cater for a crowd of 35,000. It is quite an occasion, with bookmakers dressing up in top hats and tails.

The race itself is still worth €100,000 and attracts the occasional German or British runner, with the renowned Gloucestershire trainer David Nicholson winning it twice in the 1970s with Kildagin.

It tends to be an exclusively French affair nowadays. Though none will ever match the feat of Redpath, who claimed the last of his seven victories in 1897 at the age of 21, putting even the legendary Red Rum in the shade.

LEFT: French jockey Stephane Juteau riding Alpha Speed leads over the water to win the annual Waregem Koerse, known in Belgium as the 'Grote Steeplechase van Vlaanderen', at the Gaverbeek Hippodrome, in Waregem.

Warrnambool

Victoria, Australia

Warrnambool in Victoria is the western gateway to the 151 miles of the Great Ocean Road and has its own stretch of rugged and spectacular shoreline. Southern Right Whales return each year between June and September to calve and come almost to the edge of Logan's Beach.

In the first week of May, visitors will stick around for people- and horse-watching at the Warrnambool Carnival. The three-day meeting is the nearest antipodean equivalent to the Cheltenham Festival and is home to the Grand Annual – Australia's longest, most historic and famous steeplechase.

Race meetings began almost as soon as the town was established, in this green basin a mile from the ocean. These days Warrnambool hosts around 20 fixtures per year. The large trees in the parade ring (pictured left) behind the stands are one of its more unusual features.

Australian jump racing is a minority sport compared to the Flat, now only taking place in two states, and animal rights lobbyists continue to trail Victoria. The Carnival does, though, remain a considerable tourist attraction and Grand Annual day, which closes the meeting, can draw a crowd of 13,000 with many on the natural hill grandstand behind the man-made facilities.

The Grand Annual, first run in 1872, finishes on the Flat course, an easy left-handed, mile-and-a-quarter circuit, but first passes the stands in the opposite direction and deviates onto a separate track through hilly open parkland and twisting round almost into neighbouring back gardens. Through three and a half miles, the field negotiate obstacles with Grand National-style nicknames, like the Houlahan Treble and the Mantrap. Altogether horses will jump 33 fences, three more than in the Aintree National, and believed to be the most in any world steeplechase.

Tozer Road, two small jumps either side of a path crossing, saw a nasty incident in 2011 when a loose horse called Banna Strand went over a barrier and into spectators watching from the sidelines, causing a few minor injuries. The villain of the piece made headlines for the right reasons two years later when returning for an unlikely victory in the same race.

A similarly heart-stopping incident entered jumping folklore at 'the Bool' a couple of decades earlier with the locally owned and trained Galleywood. He had fallen at the final fence in 1984 when looking the likely winner and was on the ground, covered by a screen for four minutes. Bad news seemed inevitable, but then he rose to lusty cheers from the crowd that were magnified when he had, in the words of an emotional racecourse commentator, "done a Lazarus". Two years later he won the race.

Warrnambool also played a significant part in the creation of *Waltzing Matilda*, the unofficial Australian national anthem. Christina Macpherson remembered the town band playing the Scottish tune *Bonnie Wood o' Craigielee* at the Grand Annual meeting in 1894. When Banjo Paterson was staying at her family's cattle station in Queensland the following year, she repeated it to him and he came up with the words.

BELOW: Jockey Steven Pateman riding Al Garhood clears a fence on his way to winning the Grand Annual.

Woodbine

Ontario, Canada

Racing in North America is dominated by the dirt and artificial surfaces. Any grass circuits are usually tucked away on the inside of the oval as an afterthought for the occasional races designed to attract European visitors.

They like to do things a bit differently in Canada and Woodbine is the only racecourse in North America to have a turf track on the outside. So large is this mile-and-a-half loop that the management has even experimented with running a few races clockwise in order for more of it to be used. Every other track on the continent races anti-clockwise or 'left-handed'.

Toronto's racecourse is the country's premier venue and must be one of the most utilised anywhere in the world. Between April and early December, it hosts thoroughbred meetings at least four times a week before trotting racing takes over during the winter.

Woodbine started out in a different location in 1881, at the bottom of Woodbine Avenue in a pretty spot on the shore of Lake Ontario. In 1946, the Ontario Racing Club decided to construct a modern racecourse in the north of the city to rival those in America. Slightly confusingly, it would be called New Woodbine, while Woodbine was also redeveloped and became Greenwood Raceway. Greenwood, which was visited by King George VI in 1939, survived until 1993 but is now a park and residential area. The new site has continued to enjoy Royal patronage. Queen Elizabeth II and the Duke of Edinburgh attended the Queen's Plate in 1973 and 2010.

An expensive redevelopment of the grandstands was completed in 2000 and included more restaurants and a giant floor full of slot machines, to keep constant revenue coming in. There is now a statue of Avelino Gomez, perhaps Canadian racing's most revered figure. The confident and colourful Cuban jockey bestrode the scene for 20 years but died in an accident on the track at Woodbine in 1980.

The national breeding industry is responsible for the sport's most influential modern stallion, Northern Dancer, who became the first Canadian-bred horse to win the Kentucky Derby in 1964 and returned home a national hero to win what was to be his final start, the Queen's Plate. He went to a nearby stud farm in Ontario.

Secretariat also signed off his career at Woodbine by winning the 1973 Canadian International. A year later the globe-trotting French mare Dahlia became the first European to win the same race, the country's most important prize. It is held every October alongside the prestigious E. P. Taylor Stakes.

TOP: The cup for the Queen's Plate, Canada's oldest thoroughbred horse race and the oldest continuously run race in North America.

ABOVE RIGHT: The Royal Canadian Mounted Police on ceremonial duty for the Queen's Plate.

RIGHT: The new grandstand complex was opened in 2000.

OPPOSITE: Despite the vast expanses of turf at Woodbine, the Queen's Plate is run on the dirt oval.

Worcester

Worcestershire, England

If a visitor were taken to Worcester racecourse, down the hill from Foregate Street station, past the old Royal Infirmary building now part of Worcester University, and out onto Pitchcroft, they might struggle to understand what makes it remarkable.

Certainly it is unusual to have a racecourse so close to a city centre. But lying beyond the grandstand is the reason that makes Worcester one of the most resilient racecourses to sustain horse racing for 300 years: Britain's longest river, the river Severn.

The track is one of the very oldest in the country, established just seven years after Ascot in the year 1718, and it originally held only Flat racing with several valuable events including the Worcester Gold Cup held during a summer meeting in the early nineteenth century.

The racecourse, like the nearby Worcestershire cricket ground at New Road, has always been subject to the Severn's incursions. Its shape has changed over the years, and a figure-of-eight jumps course introduced in 1880 was not welcomed by Flat trainers. It reverted to a mile-and-five-furlong oval, on a level surface with few surprises.

With the discontinuation of Flat racing in 1966, Worcester concentrated on the jumps, but a programme through the traditional winter season continued to be affected by the regular bursting of the Severn's banks.

Summer jumping was introduced in 1995 in a bid to counter this, and the season now runs from May to October, when the national racing spotlight has switched to the Flat. It means Worcester no longer holds any races of much significance but all of the top jockeys still ride there as British jumps racing ticks along year-round these days. The local council owns the land and maintains the grassland in the middle but the racecourse itself is part of the Arena management group, which took over in 2000.

As the great floods from summer 2007 attest, bad weather can appear almost unannounced. An unprecedented level of rainfall during June and July affected swathes of southern England and wiped out a heap of fixtures at both the racecourse and at the cricket ground.

RIGHT: Worcester can always be guaranteed to generate remarkable racecourse photos when the Severn bursts its banks and the rails at Pitchcroft peep above the surface of the water to delineate the track. Normally it takes place in winter, but this photo with trees in full leaf, was taken in June 2007.

Worthington Valley

Maryland, America

Fox hunting could be considered the archetypal upper-crust English pursuit but it proved to be a successful export to America. President George Washington was a fan, owning his own pack of hounds, and riders still enjoy the thrill of the chase all around the country to this day, tracking coyotes or bobcats if there are no foxes.

The pursuit germinated what has become one of America's most traditional sporting events when, in 1894, two Maryland hunt clubs, the Elkridge and the Green Spring Valley, decided to have a race through the countryside to see who was fastest. The following year members of other clubs in the state were invited to participate in the Maryland Hunt Cup and slowly the regulations have been eased so that it is now simply a contest for amateur riders, provided they have reached a certain standard.

By 1922, the Hunt Cup had a permanent home on rolling farmland in the Worthington Valley in Baltimore County. There is only the one race at the meeting, at 4pm on the final Saturday in April, around a four-mile course which is laid out every year as closely as possible to the original map.

There is jump racing elsewhere in America, over brush or hedge obstacles similar to those in Europe, but the 'timber racing' demonstrated at Worthington Valley and a few other racecourses is unique to the country. The fences are wooden posts and rails and are between 4 feet (1.2 metres) and 5 feet (1.5 metres) high.

The Hunt Cup is one of a series of timber races in Maryland across consecutive weekends in the spring, following My Lady's Manor and the Grand National at other venues in Maryland, but is considered the most difficult and prestigious. There is now a prize fund of $100,000 and a perpetual trophy which is only retired and replaced when it has been won by the same owner three times.

The whole day is quite an event for high society, with a few thousand arriving with picnics in the car, and competitors tend to be drawn from blue-chip families from the East Coast. This is not to say that the standard of riding is hopeless as the race has nurtured several jockeys, and horses, that went on to even greater glory.

One of those was Jay Trump, who was born by accident in 1957 after a mare who was believed to be sterile, Be Trump, was put out in a field with a stallion called Tonga Prince. The result of this unlikely alliance was a temperamental individual who looked a lost cause when raced on the Flat. Jay Trump ended up in the care of Crompton 'Tommy' Smith and was a revelation when tried in timber races, claiming all of the great prizes including the Hunt Cup three times. Smith's burning ambition was to win the Aintree Grand National and, under the instruction of the great English trainer Fred Winter, the pair succeeded in 1965.

Another Grand National-winning graduate of the race was Ben Nevis, who initially made little

impression when trained in England but took to American timber racing like a duck to water. He was then taken to Aintree twice, coming good at the second attempt in 1980. Charlie Fenwick, Ben Nevis's jockey, is from a family that has been intricately linked with the Hunt Cup since almost the beginning.

Women were only allowed to ride in the race by the late 1970s and 1980 saw another breakthrough when Joy Slater was the first to put her name on the roll of honour, following up in 1981 for good measure.

York

Yorkshire, England

From the late fourteenth century, the area of land just south of York's city walls, commonly known as the Knavesmire, was used for public executions. In 1739, eight years after the first race meeting had been staged there, the notorious highwayman Dick Turpin met his end on the gallows.

This Knavesmire site was not the most obvious choice for a track; it was an area of boggy land with a stream running through it. Previous venues in the historic city had been even more far-fetched, with reports of a race meeting on the frozen river Ouse in 1607.

Nonetheless, this open expanse only a few minutes' walk from central York was drained, levelled and the racecourse was constructed in a horseshoe shape. At first, like anywhere else, spectators would watch the action from the ground but by 1756, what is thought to have been the first racing grandstand anywhere in the world had been built. The designer was local man John Carr, examples of whose Palladian architecture can still be seen across Yorkshire, with a reception room and platform to view the races from above.

There have been sequences of remodelling throughout the following 250 years, some more successful than others. The bottom arcade of Carr's grandstand was the only part to survive a redesign in 1890 and it was completely moved at the beginning of the twentieth century to a spot behind the modern infrastructure. A careful recent renovation of the entire paddock area saw Carr's work restored and showcased as part of a smart hospitality area.

The place has been run by the York Racecourse Committee since 1842 and is rightfully proud of its heritage. There has still been need for it to progress, though, and some rather inferior buildings from the 1950s and 60s have been replaced by modern structures. Harmony between the old and the new has somehow been achieved and York remains comfortably in the top five of Britain's best racecourses.

In 1851 it was the site of the clash between the county's two equine titans, The Flying Dutchman and Voltigeur. The Flying Dutchman had lost his unbeaten record when failing to concede a welterweight to his younger rival in the previous year's Doncaster Cup, when some had said his jockey Charles Marlow was drunk, and there was great demand for a decider. What became known as 'The Great Match' attracted an estimated crowd of 150,000 as The Flying Dutchman exacted his revenge after an epic struggle.

There are traditionally two main fixtures at York, starting with the three days of the Dante meeting in the spring, and the main event of the Ebor meeting in August.

The summer carnival includes the Ebor itself, possibly the most important handicap race in Europe, and the Gimcrack Stakes for two-year-olds, both of which were part of the calendar before The Flying Dutchman's match. Its showpiece event is the more recent International Stakes. This race started with a bang when Roberto inflicted the only career defeat of the mighty Brigadier Gerard in 1972 and it frequently produces the highest quality event

of the entire European season, won by brilliant performers such as Dahlia, Triptych, Giant's Causeway and Frankel.

York's lofty place in the thoroughbred hierarchy saw it chosen as the temporary venue for Royal Ascot in 2005, when the Berkshire course was being redesigned. As it was only a mile and six furlongs in length the aforementioned horseshoe layout had to be closed into a loop to stage races upwards of two miles. The racecourse is perfectly level and ought to provide an ultimately fair test, but the effects of the ancient bogland have not been completely nullified and the ground can sometimes be difficult to predict.

OPPOSITE: With an attendance of more than 80,000 across the four days of the summer Ebor meeting, York's facilities are designed to cope with a big crowd.

BELOW: The Clocktower building, designed by local architects in 1922, used to serve as a board for the runners and riders but remains a cherished piece of history on the racecourse and has Listed status.

Hippodrome de Viseo

Zonza, Corsica

Europe's highest racecourse is no mere footnote in the record books; it is also surely one of the continent's most striking.

Zonza is at an altitude of 3,116 feet (950 metres) and is overlooked by the Aiguilles de Bavella, the needles of granite which are one of the most photographed attractions towards the south of the rugged island. The track is just a couple of miles from the small and pretty hilltop village of the same name.

Racing has been organized by a voluntary committee since 1928. It used to take place only once a year until 1980, when the closure of a few other Corsican racecourses meant that a few more fixtures were transferred here. They take place on Sundays between July and August, attracting a few hundred locals each time as well as tourists fortunate enough to be in the right place at the right time. Reports are that the atmosphere is relaxed, with plenty of banter and gambling.

There are no stands and punters view the action from beneath a few of the pine trees that populate this region. It is a tight and gently undulating clockwise grass circuit of only five furlongs and there tend to be five races over distances between 11 and 13 furlongs, along with two trotting heats.

Corsica is not one of the principal racing areas in France, with only a handful of tracks hosting occasional meetings. The biggest purse of the season at Zonza is €9,000 for the winner of a race confined to Anglo-Arabian cross-bred horses; a prize not to be sniffed at but small in comparison with the Parisian region.

Most of the horses are based on the island, and the events are dominated by a handful of semi-professionals. One of the leading trainers has been Christian Barzalona, grandfather of Derby-winning French jockey Mickael. As Corsica was the birthplace of Napoleon, it is an amusing coincidence that Mickael Barzalona emerged as a protégé of trainer André Fabre who has long been compared wryly with the general, not only for his diminutive stature but for his authoritative air and creation of a winning empire around the world.